David Langford took a physics honours degree at Brasenose College, Oxford and is now employed as a physicist. He has published articles on fusion power, 'bionic' cybernetics and computerised cryptanalysis, plus various science-fiction short stories. His *Twll-Ddu* won the 1977 Nova award and 1978 *Checkpoint* poll as best British amateur SF fanzine. He was on the committee of Britain's 1978 Easter SF convention and administered the International SF Awards (Hugos) for 1979. His wife Hazel is a qualified Egyptologist who has great patience with all this.

D1555846

War in 2080
The Future of Military Technology
DAVID LANGFORD

SPHERE BOOKS LIMITED
30/32 Gray's Inn Road, London WCIX 8JL

First published in Great Britain by
Westbridge Books (A Division of David & Charles) 1979
Copyright © David Langford 1979
Published by Sphere Books Ltd 1981

TRADE
MARK

Printed and bound in Great Britain by
©ollins, Glasgow

To Hazel
who as an Egyptologist
disapproves of all this

CONTENTS

INTRODUCTION
Logic of Progress

*'Tis not only the mischief of diseases, and the villany
of poysons, that make an end of us; we vainly accuse
the fury of Guns, and the new inventions of death ...*
SIR THOMAS BROWNE

There is a moment in the film *2001* which must be one of the
most disconcerting in cinema: the million-year shift from a
bone club spinning in the air to a space-station in its waltz
through vacuum. This shorthand for the whole of human
progress is all the more potent for its insistent presentation
of warfare on both sides of that temporal abyss. The bone –
with which, in the film, an unfortunate apeman has been
clubbed to death – involves a simple physics of force,
inertia and impact, at first realised only intuitively; as well
as a weapon, it is a tool. After countless millennia of
increasing knowledge and sophistication there comes the
spaceship – not overtly a weapon, but invisibly trailing its
heritage of Congreve rockets and the V-bombs of World
War II.

Science has become more closely linked with warfare as
each grows older and each encourages the other. Advanced
technology has been a military advantage for as long as
technology has existed: as when the Phoenicians and
Greeks developed the fast warship (trireme) armed with a
ram in the 8th century BC, and when centuries later the
Spartans defeated Athens largely (according to one
popular theory) because they issued their troops with up-
to-date steel weapons while other armies still kept to the
good old ways of soft iron or bronze. For a long while,
however, the military technologists stuck to an empirical

approach. A formula that worked was not to be changed. (Besides, victories were won through the glorious fighting spirit of the men themselves, plus the glorious leadership of their generals; the weapons were a small and sordid part of the process.) The point is illustrated by the legend of Damascus steel, where it was supposed to have been found empirically that a red-hot sword thrust into some unfortunate's body became harder and more durable. A scientist would at once have experimented with other means of attaining the desired temper – quenching in a pig, a dead pig, a simple bowl of water; however, the legend has it that subsequent swords were hardened in just the same fashion, since obviously the virtue of the process 'could only be' put down to the entering of the dead man's soul into the blade. The falsity of this theory is not supposed to have been exposed until it was investigated by Crusaders who happened to disagree with it on theological grounds.

Thus the attitude of the practical man – when something works or appears to work, don't monkey with it. Without any theoretical backing, early weapons evolved by a form of crude natural selection, whereby ones which were manifestly inferior were eventually discarded. Meanwhile, early philosophers who might have deduced the missing theory were overtly contemptuous of such brutish materialism. Plato turned up his nose and contemplated the Ideal; Pythagoras fiddled with mysticism and numerology, and would probably have been shocked to know the vile practical applications to which his geometry would one day be put; even Aristotle, more of a scientist than most, could dismiss actual experiment with snappy comments like: 'No man can practise virtue who is living the life of a mechanic or labourer.'

Perhaps the first real joining of scientific theory with engineering skills to a warlike end was made by Archimedes, who planned the defence of Syracuse when it was besieged by Rome in 212 BC. Archimedes thoroughly understood the principles of simple machines ('Give me a fulcrum and I will move the world') and used them to excellent effect against the Roman scaling-towers, which were easily smashed by weights dropped from the city walls. Falling weights and beams likewise broke up the flimsy ships of the invasion fleet, while simple cranes were able to grapple ships by the bows and hoist them clean out of the water. Not content with this, Archimedes is rumoured to have devised the first death-ray, in the form of a series of mirrors intended to concentrate sunlight upon enemy ships and set them afire. This seems most improbable when the target is moving at some distance, and when the mirrors are no bigger or better than could then be made – but it *is* a theoretically workable weapon devised by Archimedes out of his own head. It may even have worked on a small scale. (L. Sprague de Camp suggests that Archimedes set some disused hulk afire as an Awful Warning; J. B. S. Haldane was of the opinion that he never built the weapon but 'perhaps the Syracusan Ministry of Information dropped leaflets over the walls saying that he was going to'.)

It seems a pity that, after all these efforts, Syracuse should have fallen to a surprise attack while the good citizens were celebrating the Festival of Artemis, no doubt the equivalent of a bank holiday. The moral is plain: superior technology will not necessarily prevail against good strategy. (Nor against greatly superior numbers – Syracuse could hardly hold out forever against the Roman Empire.) Weapons technology is only the hardware of warfare; of equal importance is the software which governs its use and which takes many forms. Tight discipline, for example, which traditionally stems from the Spartans, was adopted in a softened form by Rome and finally introduced into British warfare by Cromwell. Power-politics was first encapsulated by Machiavelli in *Il Principe* (1513), while the actual theory of war 'as a continuation of politics by other means' was distilled by von Clausewitz in *On War* (1832). The more modern trend of considering strategy semi-mathematically in terms of game theory derives from von Neumann and Morgenstern's *Theory of Games and Economic Behaviour* (1947), leading to an attempt to look unblinking at nuclear hell in Kahn's *On Escalation* (1965). The present book is largely concerned with military hardware, but the hardware inevitably shapes the software – nowhere more so than in the field of actual tactics.

(Alexis Gilliland)

Advanced hardware has already had a tremendous impact on history. Greek fire is said to have helped preserve the Byzantine empire for centuries. Armour shaped the ethics of the age of chivalry by making its wearers virtually invulnerable to the unarmoured lesser breeds; this ultimate defence was eventually pierced by the English longbow, which duly became the ultimate weapon – unstoppable and long-range – until it was outranged by artillery and blocked by steel armour-plate. Now scientists and engineers are expected to display at increasingly regular intervals some new fashion in death. The examples which can be drawn from this century alone are too many to list here; some of the more significant will appear in the chapters which follow.

Before setting off on an extrapolative joyride into the military future, we must have fuel: a rich mixture of assumptions of which some may prove unrealistic. I could adopt the more doom-struck poses fashionable in recent times, and assume that our world is running down, that the energy-sources we are using will prove irreplaceable. In that case we can write *In my beginning is my end* across the history of weapons science, and contemplate a vision of the world's last warriors duelling with rusty fragments of scrap-iron amid the ash-heaps of a starved civilisation and its broken technology. This *could* be the situation in a century or less; but since it rules out technological advance, I instead offer (with head tucked firmly in the sand) Working Assumption $\tau 1$: The energy-sources now in use will not be exhausted until something equally convenient (fusion power, one hopes) has become available.

Other visions of the future familiar from science fiction include the nuclear holocaust, the world-sterilising plague, the planetary death from pollution, the natural cataclysm which shatters civilisation, and many more of an equally cheery nature. Some will be discussed later in the book, although generally in a hypothetical sense. Even if the computer-printout or the crystal ball announces positively that nuclear war will end life on Earth around the year 2000, we shall wave that aside and look still further ahead. In practice, even a nuclear exchange is unlikely to erase humanity; in the face of the worst possible war there will always be survivors, there will almost certainly be a new civilisation. Hence the optimistic Working Assumption $\tau 2$: Armageddon will never actually happen. I hope no reader will take the trouble to disprove this assumption, since there is only one way of doing so.

CHAPTER ONE

NUTS AND BOLTS

I: Generally Speaking

Join the Army . . . see the world . . . meet interesting people . . . and kill them.

T-SHIRT SLOGAN

The twentieth century has seen vast changes in the meaning of 'conventional warfare'. In older days, two armies would join battle and quite straightforwardly hack each other to pieces; the leaders would often be found within sight of the battlefront. In the late 19th century, a certain amount of sabre-work continued to take place between the volleys of bullets; this was the time recorded by Kipling, when warfare could still occasionally be treated as a game. The leaders, however, were less frequently seen in the vanguard. Since then, the personal element has steadily faded from battle, with the enemy painted more and more as a remote ogre and the leaders on either side entrenched more and more securely at home. Fighting is something to be performed by machines of the largest possible power and range. It is hardly conceivable that any importance can be attached to the arcane practice of sticking knives into people: whether called a bayonet or (more romantically) a trusty sword or halberd, the blade seems equally antique.

In World War I, however, many men died at the ends of bayonets. This was the time of the great transition from the old warfare to the new: a messy and unpleasant business. In theory, the rifle dominated the entire theatre of war, across a ravaged France; in practice, when the trenches were sunk, rifles possessed mainly nuisance value, serving only to weed out the less competent soldiers who failed to keep their heads down. In craters, ruins and folds of the mud lurked snipers, watching immobile for their chance – a hint of the guerilla wars to come. Big guns thudded monotonously behind the lines, their shells and shrapnel deadly when accurately aimed, but doing little more than smash a few men, who were quickly replaced, and a great deal of landscape, which was not.

It was a war of trenches. Each side, dug in and screened by earth and sandbags from the steady hail of bullets, constructed a maze of offensive and counter-offensive excavations in the dead land between the lines. These trenches zig-zagged across the open space (a straight line could be swept by bullets) in attempts to establish new forward lines or to undermine and blow up enemy efforts to do the same. It was dark, grimy work against an opponent who was faceless until one went 'over the top' with bayonet fixed, perhaps to return, perhaps not. Dead men lay in the open, or half-buried in craters, and no one dared retrieve them. A filthy and depressing time was had by all, and for a long while things became worse; in this war, for the first time, soldiers stared uncomprehendingly as the greenish billows of chlorine were wafted towards them on a gentle breeze.

Above all this, the happier legends were being created by pilots in flimsy wood-and-fabric aeroplanes, one-seaters and two-seaters, with a camaraderie extending even across the lines – for a time. Even when guns were mounted on the planes and pilots killed each other like common troops, there was a kind of glamour in the air. The personal element endured where the numbers were so small; the clouds were filled with individual heroes and villains, in contrast to the antlike masses who fought below. Unfortunately, this was the tiniest arena of the war. The gentleman-pilots played at chivalry, but what remained of the old honour and romance was expiring down below, lost in the cratered mud and decay, starved in that shattered wasteland that covered half of France.

World War I has receded into a historical twilight. Its images are fading – one of the few exceptions being those fragile aircraft wheeling in sunlight, high above the lines – and the present-day picture of conventional warfare owes little to this conflict, for all that the first tanks lumbered uncertainly across the battlefield in that time. The grim effects of chemical weapons and concerted shelling also became evident in World War I, but its faded atrocities have been lost in the gigantic shadow of World War II. This second Armageddon set the standard of conventional warfare for our century. The tools have improved in quality since 1945, but many of them are still recognisable; to most people, the term 'conventional warfare' means simply 'the way they used to fight in world War II' . . . anything, that is, that was done in battle between (let us say) September 1939 and 6 August 1945.

The vital image of World War II was not the trench but the armoured column. In the field, anything sufficiently important which had the temerity to stay still would be pounded by long-range and immensely accurate shells, and by the appalling bomb-power of contemporary planes. This was a war in which machines bulked ever larger and more powerful, while the ordinary soldier was often of less account. It was never entirely a battle of backrooms, of course. The idea of a war fought wholly from obscure laboratories in Nissen huts is entertaining, but unfair to those who had to carry the wonderful new weapons into action, there to find out whether or not they worked.

This at last was the war of the Scientific Method – that elusive, empirical approach which puts trust in things as they are, and discards those previous theories which have failed. (This may sound trite. But consider: *obviously* the Sun goes round the Earth. Any fool can see that! The fun comes when one tries to plot the impossibly complex orbits of the other planets about the Earth. It took centuries merely to *try* putting the Sun at the centre – and resistance to this radical new theory was quite fanatical.) Roger Bacon groped after scientific method in the Dark Ages, and centuries later Francis Bacon set it in elegant prose; upper-class gentlemen toyed with it from the seventeenth century, and its effects on warfare were felt in World War I as strange, outlandish innovations . . . the cad's trick of poison gas, the demented and vaguely unethical notion of armed and armoured vehicles. Already the Secret Weapon had a long and varied history – attach rams to the triremes and win the battle, attack the Alps with elephants (and win the hearts of the British by nevertheless losing) – but always there was this sense of the wild throw, the single stroke of genius which brings victory or defeat. In World War II the secret weapon became a matter of routine.

From the histories of that war which pack six tortured years into a few hundred pages, one feels the inexhaustible ingenuity of scientists and engineers pushed to the limit. Invention after invention lumbers forth from the mystic back rooms; *di ex machinis* on a production line. Radar, nerve-gases, infrared detection and ultraviolet signalling, sophisticated electro-mechanical cipher machines, a hundred forms of mine and booby-trap, bouncing/armour-piercing/proximity-fused/super-explosive shells and bombs, the V-bombs which towards the end were close to being spaceships . . .

Since later in this book we shall be considering the seemingly bloodless battles of a hypothetical future, this is a good point at which to recall the actual physical impact of technological warfare. The glittering game-theory world of intellect and machines, where kills are but counters swept from the board, has an unfortunate habit of intersecting the more prosaic round of human life. Ideas spring from the drawing-board into a reality of shattered flesh, fused metal, landscapes smashed to dust and blackened stumps: war. World War II saw the creation of the twentieth century's most appalling archetypes, symbols whose freight of meaning is still too heavy to bear: Auschwitz and Dachau, Cologne and Dresden – and finally the twin sunbursts which brought a lasting fame to those once obscure cities in Japan.

We are still dealing with conventional warfare, and nuclear weapons have been deported to the next chapter; but they are a prime example of the true scientific advance in weaponry. Nothing like them had ever been seen before. The same might be said of radar, and indeed of most of that war's electronic novelties. The same could not be said of every 'new' terror: the Dresden firestorm was produced by a vast tonnage of quite ordinary incendiaries, and the dreaded *Zyklon-B* of the 'final solution' was a simple compound which evolved cyanide gas. Sophistication is not required for atrocities; high-technology weapons are developed to end wars and not to make them more fearful, however much they may fail on both counts.

For new advances, in weaponry as in most fields, bring new problems to user as well as victim. In the first place, a modern weapon will generally be specialised in some way – will be inappropriate under certain fighting conditions. If everyone is armed with swords, for example, the tactics are exceedingly simple; one locates a representative enemy, inserts the sword a certain distance, and withdraws it. But a grenade capable of eliminating, say, twenty of the opposition must be expended with more care. There is the difficulty of luring twenty men to the same spot in order to avoid wasting a precious (and not at all re-usable) grenade. Variations of this problem confront any modern military force which is opposed by guerilla tactics at a lower level of technology. Advanced warfare requires massive lines of supply (the grenade must be replaced) and often vulnerable bases; but a knife needs no maintenance or ammunition, and even a rifle can fire many shots before its lurking owner must find more cartridges.

Faced with such oppostion, the US Army in Vietnam attempted several high-technology counterattacks. There was the legendary 'sniffer', a beautifully-conceived device which picked up eloctronically the very smell of the enemy — it worked well until the said enemy hung bags of urine in the trees, and filled the jungle with false alarms. The disciplined, centralised force in such confrontations has traditionally never had a satisfactory course of action in terms of combat. The resultant feeling of helpless irritation is now intensified by the certain knowledge that the foe *can* be annihilated — but at too high a price. A nuclear offensive will not only sterilise the land for which one is presumably contending, but also provoke even previous neutrals into reprisals up to and including what Herman Kahn insists on calling the 'unthinkable' option even as he thinks about it: large-scale thermonuclear war.

Besides the specialisation of tactics just noted (high technology limits you to fighting large-scale technological war: it's very difficult to go back), there is a second problem of specialisation of supply. In the simplest case, one needs the raw materials to produce the machinery of war. Thus, in World War II, Germany found herself — owing to blockades — lacking rubber desperately needed for tyres and insulation. The shortage resulted at one stage in glass beads being used for electrical insulation. Even when raw materials are available, production-lines are required to process them. A chain of processes will have weak links and a pipelene will have bottlenecks; astute enemies who attack at the right point can do damage out of proportion to the immediate destruction caused. My former college principal often told an anecdote of how in World War II he decided that ball-bearings were an especially vulnerable point in the German war effort. Bomb the ball-bearing factories and Germany would grind, so to speak, to a halt. Apparently the powers-that-be tried this advice for a time, without visible success; only when the war had finished did they learn that Germany had been reduced to a single ball-bearing factory.

II: The Basic Armoury

Point and edge, point and edge, the red water amidst of the mountains!

WILLIAM MORRIS

Is a ball-bearing a weapon? Is a cartridge a weapon, with or without its rifle? A fill survey of today's weaponry would have to cover those things which we intuitively *know* are weapons, plus any ammunition which they require, plus the supporting cast of transport, communications, detection and guidance which comes into play before the weapon strikes home – and ultimately the entire technological capability of civilisation, for virtually every aspect of technology is drawn into war. This section considers the principles of the very simplest weapons.

The first weapon to augment the human offensive capability was probably the blunt instrument still favoured in detective fiction. In *2001* the ape-Cain used a bone; a rock would have been likelier still. That bone or rock was the first means of storing energy for destructive ends. When Gerg the apeman first swung a rock, he converted muscular energy to kinetic energy (energy of motion) in the rock; in other words, the rock moved faster as he pushed it. When it coincided with a foe's skull, the energy imparted to it through Gerg's long swing of the arm was discharged in a very brief time; a shock of stunning or fatal intensity went through the victim's head. The Law of Conservation of Energy had struck! The energy would rapidly be dispersed: the stone tends to rebound slightly, the antagonist would tend to be pushed the other way, some energy would end as heat in the impacted flesh and bone . . . and so on.

Thus the simple physics behind all striking weapons – club, mace, truncheon, cosh, morningstar, quarterstaff, shillelagh, singlesticks, anything which Man's urges may prompt him to heft and swing. Golf clubs and cricket or baseball bats make fine weapons in this category.

But now the primitive warrior has meddled with the laws of motion, he is on the edge of forbidden things. What warrior does not dream of smiting his enemies at a distance? And sooner or later Gerg notices that, charged with its awful power, his rock will not cease moving when his fingers slip. When shoved in just the right way, it flies forward to strike his enemy: *magic!* The missile weapon follows inevitably from the striking weapon. Since the investment of muscular effort is stored in the rock as *kinetic* energy, energy of *motion*, it will continue to move (slowed ever so slightly by air friction) until it strikes its target or gravity pulls it in a long parabola to the ground.

The most sophisticated missile weapon seems to be the sling-shot. The sling whirls in a circle and its stone can be accelerated almost at leisure to lethal speeds – 80 kph and more. (The bolas, two rope-linked stones, can 'idle' in the same way.) This arrangement is weirdly echoed in twentieth-century particle accelerators: electronics or protons spin in a giant ring and are given an electro-magnetic push on each circuit, until finally they are released in a high-energy beam at an appreciable fraction of the speed of light. Sling and cyclotron: the same elegant concept of energy-storage is common to them both.

The next addition to this repertoire is the cutting edge. This is really one of the 'simple machines' of the old elementary physics courses: the wedge. An ideal wedge is a perfect cutting edge, the best real-life example being the razor; a variation on the principle gives us the stabbing point as in the rapier. Few weapons employ cutting or impaling in this 'pure' form; generally the edge or point is used to give extra bite – extra point, one might say – to a more massive weapon which would do damage in any case through impact but whose sharpness makes it still more devastating. Thus to the hand weapons we add various familiar items – sword, lance, halberd, dagger, trident, axe, scimitar, spear and many more. The mass of the weapon and the quality of its edge determinine 'fightworthiness'; in practice lighter weapons, or ones less subject to impact, will have the finer edges. One illustration is that anecdote of the Crusades: King Richard Lionheart swings his massive long-sword and cleaves an anvil in two, whereupon Saladin disdainfully shows how his razor-edged scimitar can slice soft cushions in mid-air. Richard's battered sword would simply knock those cushions away; Saladin's keen blade would break on the anvil. From the functional viewpoint – that of an opponent who is neither cloth nor steel – there might be little to choose between their weapons.

Sharpness is also of great value in missiles: here the point can be more important than the edge, being less likely to strike 'flat' and fail to penetrate (it also concentrates more impact at a single point). Point and edge can be combined, as in the spear, a hand-weapon which can also be flung. To the list we add the dart, throwing-knife, javelin . . .

But one thinks so naturally of the bow as a simple, fundamental weapon that it's easy to forget its difference from those so far considered. They have all been 'dynamic' weapons where motion is of the essence, where muscle-power gives kinetic energy (KE) which – unless temporarily trapped in a ring by the whirling of a sling or bolas – must at once be hurled against the target. The bow requires the fresh concept of *potential* energy (PE) – energy which is coiled, static, awaiting release. PE will change to KE unless held in check; a stone held in the air possesses gravitational PE by virtue of its height above ground, and this becomes KE – increasing speed – as the stone is allowed to fall. Picking the stone up expends muscular energy to raise its PE once more. Bending a bow stores PE in the wood, which can then spring back and impart KE to an arrow which flies we know not where (depending on our aim). The principle remains the same whether the bow is of the ordinary hand-drawn pattern or is a crossbow where a crank must be used to bend the smaller but stiffer bow. Substitute compressed air for stressed wood, and we have the airgun; substitute elastic, and the result is the familiar catapult which (according to legend) every schoolboy owns.

All these simple weapons are tools intended to deliver a burst of mechanical energy to their targets, sometimes making it more damaging by the principle of point and edge. Whether generated on the spot by muscle-power or stored as PE until the vital moment, it is KE which is unleashed upon the foe. For a moving body, the KE is given by the formula $\frac{1}{2}mv^2$ – half the mass, m, times the square of the velocity, v. The effect is increased by weilding something bigger – not of course too big to lift – or by moving it faster. (Objects of small mass can in theory be thrown very fast with little expenditure of energy – but if a human hand throws them, this too must be accelerated; even if nothing at all is held, work is done to move the hand.)

But even among simple hand weapons there are offbeat items which do not fit the categories above. A strangling-cord, for instance, is a mechanical means of changing a straight pull to a constriction; its refinement the garrotting-wire behaves like a cutting edge after the fashion of a cheesewire. (Science-fiction writers are fond of the unsupported edge of fine and unbreakable wire; if fine enough it could cut through steel with a slight pull.) The gladiator's weighted net, like the lasso, serves mainly to entangle the victim and make him vulnerable to a secondary attack. The whip – which can entangle, choke and even wound – is technically a most fascinating 'weapon': it should taper from butt to tip, and when it is shaken a wave of motion runs along its length. Energy cannot be created or destroyed; the mass of the moving section decreases with the taper as that wave moves from the butt, but the energy $\frac{1}{2}mv^2$ must stay the same and so the wave velocity increases. If the whip tapered perfectly to a point, the very tip would ultimately travel at *infinite* speed (ignoring relativity for a moment); even in this imperfect world, it does move faster than sound to produce the whip-crack. This high velocity also means that the tip can flick through skin to leave lash-wounds.

Human muscles can only do so much, and human laziness would have them do still less. It's hard work swinging a sword or bending a bow; winding a crossbow may be easier but it is also slower. There are labour-saving energy source which need no muscles to crank them, and the most easily accessible is chemical reaction energy. Even muscle-power comes circuitously from chemical interactions. Greek fire was one means of inflicting such energies upon the foe (it contained sulphur, naphtha and quicklime, caught fire when wetted and floated on water), and the history of simple combustion as a weapon probably dates back to Prometheus; the most simple, versatile and controllable source of such energy was gunpowder. One mixes saltpetre, sulphur and charcoal, applies fire and *whoof*! The mixture burns very, very rapidly. It does not explode unless confined in some way; only then can the explosive shockwave build up. Now construct a hollow tube, sealed at one end; pack in gunpowder, tampered well down and held in place with wadding upon which rests an iron ball or suitably-shaped rock; and ignite the powder through a hole in the tube. There will be an impressive explosion, and the missile will hurtle away to pay a call on the enemy. In technical terms. the gunpowder's reaction energy is transformed into KE of expansion in the hot gases produced; the pressure of these confined gases accelerates the missile on its way.

This basic system is capable of endless refinement. Loose powder is replaced by prefabricated shells (powder charge plus missile plus partial explosive containment), which are more consistent in their effects; and nowadays a breech-loading system is usually adopted so that things need not be rammed into the muzzle. Bullet-firing weapons are usually *rifled*, the inside of the barrel being carved in helical grooves to set the bullet spinning and keep it on course (the gyroscope principle – conservation of angular momentum : a spinning object will tend to stay spinning on the same axis through its own inertia, as one moving in a straight line tends to carry on in the same direction). the revolver and automatic pistol .or rifle are designed to insert fresh cartridges after firing; the machine-gun does the same continuously. More esoteric missiles are available – rifle grenades, incendiary bullets, dum-dums which fragment and tear apart their target. Larger guns fire shells especially designed to pierce armour-plate, or which are bombs in their own right. Elaborate sighting systems surround these advanced pieces of artillery; they are armoured, wheeled, camouflaged; and every one has at bottom the basic construction of a tube along which tamped explosive propels a missile.

The simplest use of explosive – the bomb – needs only a strong case and a detonator. The case may burst into shrapnel as with the hand-hurled grenade; in heavier bombs this is superfluous, since the shockwave alone can wreck buildings. Add jet-propulsion to such a bomb, and the result is a range of missiles from V-bombs to modern target-seeking SAMs. Gunpowder is now outmoded; it is called a *low* explosive suitable only to accelerate projectiles. *High* explosives would probably shatter the breech of a gun. They include TNT (trinitrotoluene), amatol (ammonium nitrate plus 20% TNT), guncotton (nitrocellulose) and the modern plastic explosives which are often quite safe to handle or even to ignite – exploding only when detonated with a high-intensity shock-wave. Another clever modern idea is plastic shrapnel, which is almost as damaging as the metal variety but cannot be detected by X-rays. Explosives are supplemented by a range of incendiaries like the infamous napalm (a jellied form of petrol).

The missile, combining bomb and delivery system, now dominates conventional warfare – even 'bomber' planes often carry missiles. In their early history, though, rockets were expensive and often more dangerous to attacker than to target; in general, they were less effective than more 'primitive' weapons like cannon. The V-1 was an effective missile without really being one in the present sense – it was a robot plane which thrummed from behind the lines, and whose engine cut out at a preset time to send it plunging like a *kamikaze* bomber to the target. Its slowness made it prey to anti-aircraft fire and the snagging cables of barrage balloons; still the V-1 was no laughing matter, being packed with a ton of high explosive. (The largest conventional bomb of that war was the UK 'Grand Slam', whose 10 tons of explosive obliterated an island of the English Channel during tests.) The V-2 superseded the V-1, being a true supersonic missile with similar explosive power; had the war gone on it might have done enormous damage. Intercontinental missiles and spacecraft later drew on the V-2 design.

Electronics also assumed great importance in World War II. Radar was developed independently on both sides; German planes flew along guiding radio beams to their targets, only to be deceived by spurious beams broadcast by the British. Guidance systems became an important part of warfare – a missile must travel far and fast, but also with accuracy. In recent fighting in the Middle East, the foot-soldier was able to take on tanks with the aid of a wire-guided missile: in one system the missile is launched from a

(*Alexis Gilliland*, from *Checkpoint*)

hand-held 'bazooka' and trails a wire carrying control information by which the soldier can guide it by eye to its target. Since such missiles typically travel at 650 kph and tank-gun shells at about 5000 kph, the advantage remains with the tank: the soldier may be dead before he can steer the missile to a hit. This situation could change as 'fire-and-forget' systems come into wider use; here the missile is laser-guided, or inertially steered by micro-computer, or simply homes in on hot objects (jet exhaust) or metallic objects (tank armour).

To complete this rapid tour about today's conventional

arsenals, there is the CBW department: Chemical and Biological Warfare. These weapons do not rely on delivery of energy, but work directly upon the machinery of life. They cannot be used against structures, as even napalm can – only against people and their food-supplies. This makes them an object of particular horror; this is their appeal to the economic strategist. How exquisite to erase the enemy and leave his goods intact!

Chemical warfare is the more controllable of this sinister pair; a gas can be released in one area to disperse harmlessly in time. Liquids – such as defoliants – can be sprayed still more precisely, but most chemical weapons are gases or dispersed materials (aerosols, impalpable powders) which behave like gases. Chemical weapons are not that novel: the chlorine used in World War I (which destroys the respiratory tissues and fills the lungs with weeping fluid) could have been deployed in the Crimean war, but was then thought too dreadful to use. It has been discarded in favour of later brews, since men can easily be masked against it and its potency falls rapidly with dilution. Also obsolete are the vesicant or blistering gases like mustard-gas (dichlorodiethyl sulphide) and Lewisite. 'Safe' gases which attack the eyes and upper respiratory system – tear-gas, Mace – have a limited war potential, being used mainly in riot-control and against besieged criminals in what we call peacetime. Other gases can block the oxygen-carrying capacity of the blood, the classic examples being the cyanide compounds. Victims gasp for breath and inhale great gulps of pure air, which does no good since their blood has been made incapable of taking up oxygen.

J. B. S. Haldane suggested that mustard-gas was the most humane weapon ever devised, since only 2·6% of casualties were killed and 0·25% permanently incapacitated, while high explosives and shrapnel kill or maim about half their victims. But a drifting gas-cloud can claim more victims over a wider area than a shell.

The nerve gases are unquestionably deadly. The German gases Tabun and Sarin struck at the enzyme cholinesterase, essential to the transmission of nerve-impulses; the victim's body became a country in anarchy, its lines of communication cut. Less than a milligram of Sarin leads to coma, convulsions and death. Absorption takes place through skin as well as the moister membranes; gas-masks can only delay it. A city of half a million people could in theory be depopulated with under 500 grams of Sarin; in practice, fortunately, much of the gas is 'wasted' and hundreds of tons would be required. (By 1945 Germany had stockpiled enough to wipe out thirty large cities, even allowing for wastage.) Still higher levels of toxicity are attained in modern nerve-gases like VX, details of which tend to be classified. Roughly, 250 tons of VX released over a city could cause as many deaths as a 5-megaton H-bomb. Another improvement is the binary gas, whose two components are individually harmless and must be mixed prior to release. Unpleasant though gas-warfare seems, it is at least reassuring to know that stockpiles need not be dangerous.

Biological weapons are harder to control unless of a very simple nature – like early 'poisoned' weapons where the point or edge was made so insanitary that a wound would probably pick up a fatal infection. Large-scale biological weapons – mutated bacterial plagues – will make equally enthusiastic inroads on friend and foe alike. Naturally there will be attempts to have vaccines or antibiotics available to protect one's own side – but there is no guarantee that fast-breeding micro-organisms will not develop mutant forms immune to these defensive measures. A risky business, but again so *economical*. Tons of gas and megatons of explosive are equally unnecessary:

one man could spread disease across a country, a single aricraft could spray it over thousands of miles. Bacteria are efficient killers; the botulinus bacterium (*Clostridium botulinum*) manufactures as a metabolic waste the most lethal poison known. A couple of pounds of botulinus toxin could destroy a race; and each individual specimen of the fast-breeding, easily cultured bacterium produces the toxin constantly. In World War II this weapon, like nerve-gss, was left unused for fear of equally frightful reprisals. The same fears may deter the owners of whatever new bugs military bacteriologists have now produced.

In a way, CBW has come to a dead end. Nerve-gases can eliminate whole populations – but how to deliver them? The problem is no longer one of chemistry; gas-carrying missiles must pierce a country's defences, cylinders must be smuggled in for dumping in reservoirs, troops must be protected against the vapours they disseminate. With micro-organisms there is little point in increasing dead-liness; what's needed is a means of making the bugs tell friend from foe.

Despite such arsenals, military actions are ironically restricted to weapons close to those of World War II – rifles, artillery, missiles. Improvements of quality are tolerated: the precision-bored rifle is fitted with image-intensifier sights for aim in near-darkness, the missile carries as much electronics as explosive and seeks its target with radar eyes. More exotic weaponry is avoided for fear of escalation, the bigger-and-better syndrome which leads rung by rung up Kahn's ladder to all-out nuclear war. The mushroom clouds still cast long shadows from 1945; nobody cares to cross the nuclear threshold and fight with weapons too powerful to comprehend.

III: Adapting to Space

Every body remains in a state of rest or of uniform motion in a straight line, unless it is compelled by impressed forces to change that state.

Change of motion is proportional to the impressed force, and takes place in the direction of the straight line in which that force is impressed.

Action and reaction are equal and opposite and act on different bodies.

SIR ISAAC NEWTON

Nuclear weapons are also feared for their novelty. The CBW laboratory contains more frightful powers, but its history stretches far back to poisons and those deliberately unhygienic blades. In nuclear war, moreover, there is the additional fear of long-term hazards from fallout. For such reasons nuclear tests have been banned (the signatory powers having tested all they wish) in Earth's atmosphere and the 'international ground' of Antarctica. Underground tests are presently still permissible, and countries like China which are not signatories to the test-ban treaty retain the option of exploding nuclear devices in their own airspace. Outer space is also held to be a prohibited zone as regards testing – and so any skirmish Out There is liable to be was determinedly non-nuclear as the limited wars below. So it's interesting to consider the effectiveness of more primitive weapons in the unfamiliar environments of space.

Consider a hand-to-hand struggle in free-fall, to be fought for some reason with the simplest tools or weapons. Combatants naturally wear spacesuits, offering some protection against harm; but a very small leak can cause incapacitation (and hasty fumbling for sealing patches!)

while damage to the helmet or faceplate will almost certainly mean death. In the free-fall arena, striking weapons like the club behave oddly. A club is most effective in the downward blow, combining the acceleration due to gravity with that from the attacker's muscles; in free-fall the club has all its mass but no weight – no tendency to fall. Blows at all angles become equally effective, there being no 'down'. A problem is that as our spaceman swings his club, the rest of his body will tend to swing in the opposite sense. Apply force to an object and it's pushed away; symmetrically, you also push yourself away from it. On Earth, gravity holds you down and friction stops you slipping; in free-fall neither force is present. The club swings in a wide clockwise arc; to compensate, the attacker's body moves slowly anticlockwise, the body mass being greater than that of the club and the speed correspondingly less. If an attacker is foolish enough to try swinging a really massive 'weightless' object like a steel girder, the girder will move only slightly while he'll probably throw himself, spinning, clean out of the fight. One must take care with massive weapons. Even when the attacker manages to hit his victim, the impact will set them moving apart so they must now get back in range for the next round. This is one reason why all the best science-fiction spacesuits have little manoeuvring jets.

Smaller missiles can be flung successfully – indeed, the absence of air and gravity is a positive boon, since without external forces or air-friction the missile will travel in an undeviating line to its target. (This is true if the battle is remote from any planet. In orbit, although the situation is technically one of free-fall, the acceleration of a missile will shift it out into a new orbit – not a straight line.) The thrower, meanwhile, moves in the opposite direction; unless he threw the missile along a line passing through his own centre of mass, the off-centre force will set him slowly rotating. He can hurl another stone in the opposite direction to cancel (approximately) the unwanted momentum; but the only practical solutions are little jets or anchorage to some massive object. Without such anchorage a slingshot is not to be advised; one imagines an interesting rotating system, with the sling-wielder and his stone spinning in opposite directions – no doubt to the detriment of aim.

These difficulties of Newtonian mechanics are inevitable with massive weapons that crush or break. It's logical to introduce finesse *via* lighter weapons which harm by point and edge. Either as a reaction against super-technology and planet-busting or through sheer love of the romantic, several science-fiction writers have worked such weapons into their future scenarios. Examples are E. E. Smith's *Lensman* series, Charles Harness's *The Paradox Men* and Frank Herbert's *Dune*: each includes the gimmick of an 'energy screen' which typically stops bullets and more exotic attacks while being pierced by slow-moving objects. Smith then introduces parties of 'Valerians' with 'space-axes', Herbert offers outlandish knives, and Harness makes unabashed use of the rapier. This is partly the tongue-in-cheek approach which gave us the celebrated space-pirate boarding a ship with a slide-rule between his teeth . . . but such weapons as the rapier might be surprisingly effective in free-fall combat, despite incongruous associations ('And then, Athos, I pinked him thrice in the oxygen regulator'). Rapiers have low mass, yet a hit anywhere could be deadly in space. A space-going Saladin's scimitar could make a few deft slashes while Richard Lionheart struggled with the difficulties of swinging his great sword and himself simultaneously.

So far we have mainly considered the absence of gravity. The absence of air also has its effects. A boomerang could certainly be thrown, but would lose all its aerodynamic

support and travel in a straight line rather than the familiar curve; nor, save by a lucky bounce, would it return. Flighted missiles like darts and arrows would be deprived of their ability to maintain orientation; with no drag on the flights, they would turn slowly end-over-end in flight, with only a small chance of the business end striking the target. Arthur C. Clarke solved the problem in his short story 'Robin Hood FRS': the bow is rifled, setting the arrows spinning about their long axis as they depart. The gyroscopic principle already mentioned will make them resist the urge to turn end-over-end; they will merely 'wobble' or precess in their flight, while travelling indefinitely in a dead-straight line.

Gas-propulsion weapons like the airgun – or for that matter the peashooter and blowpipe – must be provided with a compressed-gas supply. The presence of air is unimportant with airgun pellets – indeed, it slows them down; with darts, rifling is required. But airguns are more complex mechanisms with moving parts, and could become unreliable in space. Metal parts can cold-weld together in vacuum at low temperatures; lubricating oils evaporate or freeze; the sizes of parts may change beyond acceptable limits. If a space-chilled weapon is taken 'indoors', corrosive water will condense within it. Matters become still worse with weapons using explosives.

Gunpowder and explosives *will* operate in space; such compounds contain their own oxygen and burn too fast to take note of external supplies. Firing a pistol or rifle is similar, mechanically, to throwing a rock – the attacker is pushed backwards by the recoil. Meanwhile, the gun is heated and metal parts expand – perhaps it jams, since hot expanded metal and metal at sub-zero temperatures now form part of the same mechanism. Hairline cracks result from too-rapid temperature changes. Perhaps the explosive will fail, partially decomposed by the effects of alternating vacuum and 'indoor' pressure, or partially evaporated into the sucking emptiness of space. It could become dangerously unstable, whole clips of cartridges detonating at once . . . Guns tend to unreliability down on Earth; to make them function in space could take long years of research.

Bombs are indifferent to zero-gravity; as mentioned above, high explosive carries its own air-supply. But the lack of air reduces a bomb's destructive radius. Air transmits the sharp, deadly shockwave of an exploding bomb; in vacuum the effects are entirely confined to the expanding gases. These remain destructive at close range (and shrapnel at any range), but, at a distance where in air the shockwave would be crushing, there is merely a gale of gas dispersing into space, capable of nothing more than a push.

An infinitude of unlikely battlegrounds can be imagined

– some more likely than others. Low gravity produces less change than free-fall; antagonists can leap high in the air or heft a club larger than could be carried in normal gravity. There are compensating hazards: the high leap leaves one virtually helpless until the descent, and there's little virtue in a massive club without the help of high gravity to bring it smashing down on enemy skulls; the wielder is more likely to be despatched by a swifter opponent as he swings. Once again Saladin's light, sharp scimitar has the advantage of Richard's massy sword. The word 'massy' is used advisedly, as mass does not change while weight is a measure of the gravitational force. Any sword would be 'weighty' on Jupiter, and especially Richard's, though it is equally 'massy' everywhere. Probably in Jupiter's high gravity the 'weightiness' would be so great that Richard could scarcely *lift* his sword – Saladin wins again.

Low gravity implies a small world: minor planet, moon, asteroid. Ben Bova in *The Duelling Machine* imagines a tiny world where it's inadvisable to leap too high since escape velocity is only a few kilometres per hour and excessive enthusiasm would mean the jumper never came down. (Earth's escape velocity is about 40,000 kph and the Moon's 8500 kph – followers of Apollo missions will recall the contrast between the vast rockets which blasted the astronauts free of Earth and the almost anticlimatic departure of the Lunar Module from the Moon's surface – balanced on a puny-looking jet and shedding aluminium foil as it rose.) With really low escape velocity, Bova's interesting strategy is possible: one allows the foe to hurl rocks and merely concentrates on dodging them until one of his own missiles – sent into close orbit by the force of the throw – circumnavigates the little world and hits him in the back.

So the combat environments become more fantastic, the hazards more esoteric and the tactics more improbable. It's time to consider in more detail the sophisticated weaponry available or under development today. The world's vast nuclear arsenals deserve close study, looming as they do over every present-day military action; beyond are weapons which are only slowly emerging from the mists of fantasy and prediction – lasers, and partial-beam weapons, and others which may never materialise but must be considered – just in case.

CHAPTER TWO

NUCLEAR WAR

I: The Energy of the Nucleus

MOLECULE, n. The ultimate, indivisible unit of matter. It is distinguished from the corpuscle, also the ultimate, indivisible unit of matter, by a closer resemblance to the atom, also the ultimate, indivisible unit of matter . . . The ion differs from the molecule, the corpuscle and the atom in that it is an ion.

AMBROSE BIERCE, *The Devil's Dictionary*

The definition above is still a fair guide to nuclear physics as expounded by the daily newspapers – although the notion of an ultimate, indivisible unit of matter is out of favour. Instead we have a collection of fuzzy little indeter-minate things which can never – even in principle – be brought quite into focus. Fortunately, atoms can be described *via* models like the famous miniature solar system with planetary electrons orbiting a central nucleus of tight-packed protons and neutrons. This gives some informa-tion, as a sketch-map tells something about a country; but 'the map is not the territory'. Confusion of map and territory is easily avoided on the larger scale – here is the map and there the territory, which obviously has qualities not shown in the map. Atoms are not available for such comparison . . . no one has really *seen* one. We can guess at their arrangement, setting the pattern by X-ray diffraction darkly; we follow their paths as vapour-trails in the cloud chamber. But, unless today's physics is fundamentally wrong, no one can ever look through some super-microscope to see the structure of a single atom (and perhaps say: 'Good grief, it looks like a tiny solar system after all'). Our mathematical map of electron orbits does not show motion in such and such a path; it only gives the *probability* that an electron will be at a given place. There is a distribution of probability through space – a distribution of the electron itself through space – and confronted with the complex patterns involved, even physicists will often think of the electron as a little ball orbiting its nucleus. The important point is that this is not the *whole* truth . . . and neither will be the descriptions of nuclear events which follow.

Physics has spawned countless 'fundamental particles', many so ephemeral that a lifetime of thousand-millionths of a second qualifies a particle as 'stable'. We need consider only the familiar electron, proton and neutron. Electrons are light particles (leptons) with a single negative charge; protons are heavy particles (or baryons) with a mass 1840 times that of the electron; neutrons are also baryons with similar mass but no charge whatever. All are 'stable', although *solitary* neutrons tend to split after several minutes into an electron and a proton. In the simple model the nucleus is a superdense mass of nucleons – protons and neutrons – with electrons buzzing around outside. An atom's chemical properties depend almost entirely on the number of protons (Z) in the nucleus; this *atomic number* is so important that there's a unique name for every kind of atom, corresponding to Z. For $Z = 1$ the name is hydrogen, for $Z = 2$ helium, and so on through the elements. N, the total number of nucleons (protons and neutrons), determines the atomic mass and is called the mass number. Atoms with the same Z but different N (i.e., ones differing only in the number of neutrons) are called isotopes; thus U-235 ($Z = 92$, $N = 235$) and U-238 ($Z = 92$, $N = 238$) are isotopes of uranium. Finally, to unravel the confusion of definitions quoted above: a *molecule* is two or more atoms electrostatically joined, an *ion* is an atom which has gained or lost electrons and thus has an overall electrical charge, and the *corpuscle* is a term no longer used by physicists.

When discussing nuclear effects we usually forget orbital electrons; the forces and energies of the nucleus are so much greater. Electrons can be wrenched free from metals at the cost of a certain amount of energy, usually in the range 10 to 100eV. One eV is one electron volt, the energy acquired by an electron accelerated through a potential of one volt. A 1-gram weight travelling at 1cm per second would have a KE of around 600,000,000,000 or 6 $\times 10^{11}$eV, also written as 600,000MeV or 60 GeV.) To wrench a nucleon from its nucleus would take more like 8 or 9MeV. The proportional difference is like that between lifting a man and lifting his handkerchief. The lesser, electronic forces are responsible for all chemical bonds; the vastly greater nuclear forces are our concern, though electrostatics still has its part to play.

Nature has four known interactions – four ways for things to attract or repel each other. These, in decreasing order of strength, are the strong nuclear, the electromagnetic, the weak nuclear and the gravitational interactions. Their 'coupling constants' illustrate the relative strengths – respectively about 1, 0·0073, 5 $\times 10^{-14}$ and about 10^{-39}. Gravity is the weakest despite its significance on Earth; when you lift an object, chemical – electromagnetic – effects in a few ounces of muscle are overcoming the gravitational pull of *the entire Earth*. A concentration of charge as vast as this concentration of mass is virtually impossible – the tremendous repulsive forces would blow it apart.

The strong nuclear force could pull all the matter in the Universe into one tiny lump, were it not that this force is short-range – it functions only over distances even smaller than typical nuclear sizes, thus holding nuclei together without having much effect outside – it is electromagnetic forces which hold electrons in their orbits. So the nuclear charge is positive (Z units of charge, one for each proton) – and like charges repel. The nuclear force holds the nucleus together, electromagnetic forces strive to push it apart. These are the main effects which give shape to the curve of binding energy (fig. 1).

The 'binding energy per nucleon' is the energy we must supply to pull one nucleon completely free of the nucleus. The higher the binding energy, the more stable the element. There is no binding energy for ordinary hydrogen; the nucleus is a single proton unbound to anything else. Deuterium ('heavy hydrogen') has one proton and one neutron, linked by the strong interaction; it has a binding energy which must be supplied if the two nucleons are to be parted. As N rises, so at first does the binding energy per nucleon since up to a point each nucleon attracts all the others. The electromagnetic force which is pushing them apart also grows with the number of protons. When the nucleus reaches a certain size it becomes too large for the strong force to reach right across; nucleons are linked only to those nearby. But the electromagnetic force is long-range; each proton still pushes against all the others. At the right of the curve, binding energies are low because the electromagnetic push is weakening the nuclear bonds; at the left, binding energies are again low because there are fewer nucleons to form the strong bonds. The most stable elements are at the top of the curve around mass-number 60 – elements like iron, cobalt and nickel. (In science fiction, both E. E. Smith and Alfred Bester have slipped up using the super-stable iron as a nuclear fuel.)

The irregularities at the left of the curve have to do with the groupings of nucleons within a nucleus. Briefly, isotopes with mass-numbers which are multiples of 4 are often unusually stable with a high binding energy – hence

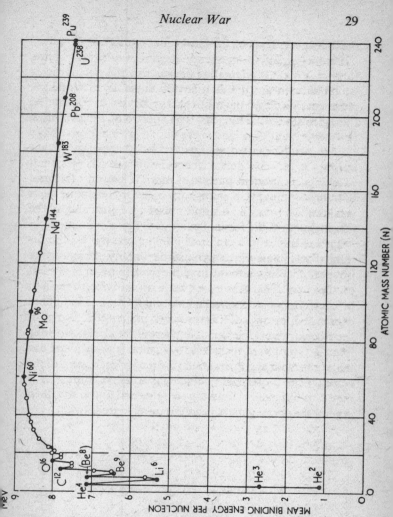

Fig. 1. Nuclear binding energies for the most stable form of each element. Note the peaks of stability for helium-3, carbon-12 and oxygen-16. Beryllium-8 *should* be stable but in practice flies apart to give two helium nuclei.

the 'unexpected' peaks for He-4, C-12 and O-16.

Binding energy is an energy deficit – a nucleus has less total energy than originally possessed by the free particles which make it up (unless it is very unstable). This deficit represents stability: the more energy needed to disperse it, the more stable the nucleus. The spectre of Einstein now reminds us that mass and energy are equivalent: an object cannot have negative energy and so the energy deficit appears as a mass deficit. The nucleus weighs less than would its component parts – or more if it is unstable and has *surplus* energy, a mass *excess*, as for example does uranium. To break up a stable nucleus we must supply the missing mass in the form of energy.

Look again at the curve of binding energy. To the far right are elements which are unstable – many of them break up spontaneously into more stable nuclei further to the left on the curve. This is radioactive decay. Moving to the left, binding energy grows; when an atom splits, this difference of energy appears as KE in the fragments. In effect, some of the nuclear mass has become energy. Similarly, working from left to right of the curve, by fusing light nuclei we can make a heavier and more stable nucleus (closer again to the central peak of the curve) which has a high binding energy and thus weighs less than the two original nuclei together. Again, the missing mass becomes pure, free energy.

II: The Fission Bomb

*If every two inches of the circumference of the
matter of the world possessed 1⅔ drams of Radium,
the total amount would be 2,737,152,000 drams;
this would give us 8,811,456,000 scruples of Radium
to every two inches of Earth's energy.*
T. O'MAHONEY, *Philosophy of God's Mathematics
of the Atomic Energy*

An ounce of uranium, completely fissioned into lighter and
stabler elements, would have in theory the explosive power
of some 600 tons of TNT. But, whatever the energy
released, it helps little to know that a molecule of some
potential high explosive will break down to give off heat.
From considerations of energy, ordinary sugar would be a
possible explosive since great heat is given off as it burns. In
the same way, the nuclear conversion from mass to energy
is no weapon unless very many nuclei can be fissioned in a
short time. Radioactive materials like natural uranium
normally suffer slow, continuous disintegration; a lump of
uranium is always faintly warm, but the death-dealing
possibilities are not obvious. What is needed is a chain-
reaction which will spread like a forest fire – but far faster –
among the nuclei. When Einstein (egged on by US
physicists Szilard, Teller and Wigner) told all this to
President Roosevelt in 1939, no one knew whether the
chain-reaction was possible.

It *was* known that uranium emits neutrons in spontaneous fissions; in theory these neutrons could be used to
trigger further fissions. Since more than one neutron is
emitted – about two-and-a-half on average – in each
fission, the reaction could grow rapidly. The Manhattan

Project found that of the two uranium isotopes U-235 and U-238, only the former was suitable for weapons. The latter formed more than 99% of all natural uranium.

When U-235 absorbs a neutron it becomes for an instant the highly unstable U-236. This isotope would appear well below the line of the binding-energy curve, which is based on the most stable isotope(s) of each element. Almost instantly, the U-236 nucleus flies apart into two smaller and more stable nuclei, plus up to three neutrons, plus a blast of gamma radiation. The radiation is part of the released energy, the rest being KE in the neutrons and fission fragments. If the piece of U-235 involved is small, the fission neutrons may escape; if it's sufficiently large (above 'critical mass'), they're more likely to strike other U-235 nuclei which explode in their turn. The chain reaction can grow exponentially (fig. 2) until so much energy is released that the original lump of U-235 is vaporizwd. Then the dispersal of the matrial will increase the average distance between nuclei and eventually cut off the chain-reaction – the neutrons being unlikely to score a hit.

Obviously the 'critical mass' depends not only on the amount but the shape of the material. A long thin rod would allow neutrons to leak out all along its length, and only those travelling along the rod would be very likely to encounter a U-235 nucleus. A sphere is the best shape of all, having the minimum surface (leakage) area for its volume and needing the smallest amount of U-235. Uranium is not the only usable fissile material – by 1943 an alternative, plutonium-239, was being manufactured from U-238 in purpose-built reactors. Since a critical mass will go off of its own accord, triggered by spontaneous fission or by a stray neutron from the air, it is also necessary to prevent criticality from being reached until the right moment. The chain reaction is then encouraged with a flood of 'priming' neutrons from some external radiation source.

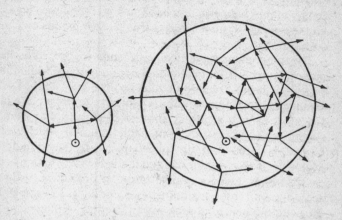

Fig. 2 As the sphere of fissile material is made larger, the proportion of neutrons colliding to result in fissions, rather than merely escaping, increases. This is because the surface of a sphere is $4\pi r^2$ and its volume $4/3\pi r^3$, so that by doubling the radius r we increase the quantity of fissile material 8 times while increasing the surface area only 4 times. (Adapted from S. Glasstone, *The Effects of Nuclear Weapons*.)

There are many misconceptions of criticality. One is spoofed in a piece by Kevin Smith: his villain posts parcels of Pu-239 to his chosen victim. When enough have arrived on the door-mat, criticality is achieved and the plutonium npile erupts in a titanic nuclear explosion. (Luckily the victim 'had dropped his pencil between two blocks and the graphic therein was absorbing just enough neutrons to prevent the holocaust'.) In real life Pu-239 itself resists being brought to criticality! As that pile of ingots grew, it would behave like a reactor and grow warmer. As criticality came close, a limited chain reaction would begin and the Pu-239 would grow hot – melt – and flow across the floor into a non-critical shape. If contained in a vat or crucible, its heat of reaction would boil it away. The very energy of the chain-reaction has a strong tendency to break up the reacting system *before* a true nuclear explosion can develop.

Thus a bomb must use violent measures to force its fissile material into supercriticality and hold it in place while the enormous heat of reaction builds up. The US 'Thin Man' arrangement used conventional explosive to fire a piece of U-235 as if from a gun at another piece; the 'Fat Man' system contained a sphere of fissile material which was blasted inwards – made to collapse – by surrounding explosive. Between explosive and fissile shell was a 'tamper' casing which served a double purpose, providing further containment for the fissioning mass and *reflecting* some of the escaping neutrons back inward, reducing the leakage and thus the actual mass required.

The first test bomb was exploded at Alamogordo (New Mexico) on 16 July 1945. The results were satisfying and terrifying: a fireball hundreds of metres across and 'brighter than a thousand suns' with a temperature of 300,000°C, a blast which literally shook the Earth for kilometres around and bounced test instruments metres into the air, a mushroom-shaped cloud thousands of metres high. The equivalent in terms of ordinary explosives was about 20,000 tons of TNT. The V-bombs which nearly demoralised London, and were able to annihilate half a street, carried only *one* ton of explosive. The payloads of all the V-bombs launched during World War II totalled less than 10,000 tons.

Two more fission bombs of similar power were available, one uranium ('Little Boy') and one plutonium ('Fat Boy'). 'Little Boy' never reached Hiroshima when dropped there on 6 August 1945; a radar-echo device exploded it 570 m over the city. Impact-fusing was unsuitable for a precision-crafted nuclear device (whose explosive must go off in just the right way), and more devastation can be achieved from above with such explosions, less energy being wasted on land and air.

The first damage was done by the 'heat-flash' – direct radiant energy from the fireball, of such intensity as to blind (temporarily, as a rule) anyone looking up. During atmospheric tests, sunglasses were compulsory – sunglasses so nearly opaque that wearers saw nothing but the Sun itself, dimly, and the man-made sun which briefly lit up the landscape. The fireball does not appear instantaneously but grows from a point of intolerable fire to its full diameter of perhaps 300 m within less than a second. Besides visible light, it emits heat sufficient to cook flesh at close range, plus X-rays and gamma-rays whose effects will later plague the survivors (if any). Moments after the flash follows the blast – a shockwave whose relentless force literally flattened the centre of Hiroshima. From an air-blast the shockwave is an expanding sphere which smashes vertically downwards immediately below the fireball, at 'ground zero'; as this sphere grows and intersects the ground on a wider front, a circle of diminishing destruction races out towards the suburbs of the target city. Meanwhile, tremendous heat has been expended on the empty air, which rises; winds rush in from every quarter, whipping the ionised gas of the fireball into a rising column of flame and smoke which spreads in the upper air to a mushroom-shaped cloud. Long afterwards, by-products of the chain reaction and the remainder of the unused fissile material will settle as fall-out.

Nagasaki met its fate a few days after Hiroshima, the supposed intention being to convince Japan that many more nuclear weapons were in store. This may or may not have hastened the Japanese surrender. It is difficult to comment on the prayer offered to speed the Nagasaki bomber on its way, which ran in part: 'Give to us all the courage and strength for the hours that are ahead; give to them rewards according to their efforts. Above all else, our Father, bring peace to Thy world . . .'

Uranium and plutonium bombs were built simultaneously because, working against time, Manhattan Project scientists dared not abandon any hopeful line of research. Uranium bombs required the tedious separation of U-235 from U-238; as isotopes of the same element they are chemically identical and separation must rely on the tiny difference in atomic mass. The favoured method involved gaseous uranium hexafluoride (UF_6); U-235 hexafluoride diffuses through porous material slightly faster than U-238 hexafluoride, and so the U-235 is labouriously concentrated. Plutonium exists in nature only in minute amounts, the result of neutron capture in U-238; it had to be extracted from 'spent' but highly active reactor-fuel rods. With today's plenitude of reactors, plutonium is the standard weapon material; those without reactors must extract U-235 using a centrifuge method developed in 1960. The typical nuclear-fission weapon of today is essentially a sphere of chemical explosive whose detonation collapses a fissile core. But this 'pure' fission bomb is not used as such, although amateurs or terrorists might build one – the nuclear equivalent of the sugar-and-weedkiller bomb. Plutonium fission is now merely the match or percussion cap to detonate the far more potent fusion bomb.

III: Fusion and After

'. . . I've often thought that the last day will be brought about by some colossal boiler heated to three thousand atmospheres blowing up the world.'

'And I bet the Yankees will have a hand in it,' said Joe.

JULES VERNE, *Five Weeks in a Balloon*

In uranium fission, mass is converted to destructive energy; the amount varies, since U-235 can split in various ways to give a variety of fragments. Typically the energy release is some 200 MeV per fission, representing around 0·1% of the atomic mass. If hydrogen atoms undergo *fusion* to become helium, the release is closer to 0·5% of the mass. This suggests a more efficient, economical bomb: hydrogen is exceedingly cheap and its rarer isotope deuterium is still much cheaper than purified U-235 or synthetic Pu-239. Fusion also hints at a power-source considerably cheaper than fission reactors; but (human nature being what is is) the bomb was studied first.

The hydrogen isotopes are ordinary hydrogen H-1, whose nucleus is a single proton, deuterium H-2, which has an added neutron, and tritium H-3 with two extra neutrons: they are also known as H, D and T. All three can take part in fusion: two protons can fuse and (emitting a positron – positive electron – to shed excess charge) become a deuteron or D nucleus; D and T can fuse in more than one way to generate He-4 plus an odd proton; two D nuclei can fuse to He-4 directly. He-4 has a high binding energy, making it an energetically useful end-product of hydrogen fusion.

But how are nuclei persuaded to fuse? In fission, neutrons spread like an infection from nucleus to nucleus as the chain reaction grows; in fusion, the nuclei themselves must be forced together. Their positive charges repel and oppose this, in contrast to the uncharged fission neutron which steals through an atom like a thief in the night; to pierce the electrostatic barrier, the attacking nucleus must travel very fast indeed so as to push through to within range of the strong nuclear forces. High-voltage accelerators can fling deuterons at a tritium-impregnated target fast enough for fusion, although not on the lavish scale required for a bomb or reactor – or a cigarette-lighter, for that matter: in such experiments the target is heated far more by the deuteron beam energy than by the few puny fusions caused.

To make large numbers of nuclei collide, we heat them. The energy added to heated hydrogen becomes KE of the atoms, which rush about violently, bouncing off one another's electrostatic armour. The violence of such collisions will not force protons together on any reasonable scale below temperatures of the order of millions of degrees; this reaction is workable only in places like the core of the sun. On Earth we fall back on more easily triggered reactions – the D-D reaction between two deuterons or the expensive though lower-temperature D-T reaction of deuteron and triton. Now temperatures of only a few hundred thousand degrees are necessary. There is also a sort of chain-reaction effect in that each fusion releases energy which speeds up the nuclei still more, increasing the rate of fusion.

The high temperatures required are available in an ordinary fission explosion. (This perishes one dream of the 'clean' fusion bomb which discards the deadly heavy-metal fuels like uranium which lead to lingering fall-out.) The first thermonuclear explosion – so called from the vast heat of triggering – was set off by a fission bomb in liquified D-T 'fuel'. This was in 1952 at a coral atoll called Eniwetok. The blast had the effect of 10,000,000 tons of TNT, or 10 megatons; Hiroshima was hit with just 20 kilotons. Little of the atoll remains.

The nuclear technicians had barely started. Next came a replacement for the refrigerated D-T mixture: the solid compound lithium deuteride, a highly convenient fusion fuel still in use. This works as follows: lithium-6 can absorb a fission neutron from the trigger explosion, breaking down to He-4, T and a not-to-be-despised 4·8 MeV of energy. In the heat of the fission bomb, the D in the compound goes into D-D and D-T reactions to produce still more energy. Thus the fusion bomb becomes relatively cheap (no expensive tritium) and convenient (no need to include a refrigerator).

With the power of a 10-megaton device to hand, the technicians did not pause. They now considered the 'wasted' neutrons emitted from the fusion bomb. Certainly these could kill people, but with ingenuity they could be used to kill many more people. U-238, previously useless in weapons, *can* be fissioned by sufficiently fast neutrons, as produced in plenty by a fusion bomb. By surrounding the entire explosive core of a fusion bomb with U-238, a large explosive boost was derived from a relatively cheap material. Thus the Bikini bomb of 1954, with an explosive force of 15 megatons. Thus also the discontinuous swimsuit named after this test-site, which was declared to have a 15-megaton effect upon the male libido: a sentiment open to doubt.

Such fission-fusion-fission weapons are now widely used – or, rather, widely stockpiled. In search of the bigger, cheaper bang, fusion's supposed advantage of cleanliness has been enthusiastically sacrificed: the uranium-fission boost gives extremely 'dirty' fall-out which can linger in the

air for weeks, and for years in soil or human bone-marrow.
Now, although USSR bombs approaching 100 megatons
have been tested, there seems little point in bigger weapons.
One can strike more flexibly with 50 one-megaton bombs
than with one of 50 megatons; and, with the fear of
interceptors and 'pre-emptive disarming attack', it is
strategically better to keep many nuclear eggs in widely
separated baskets. Recent work on actual weapons – as
opposed to defence, evasion and delivery – has concentrated on small 'tactical' weapons, often having an amount
of fissile material which cannot ever go critical until
explosively super-compressed and encouraged by neutron-
reflecting materials. Yields of a few kilotons are normal;
they can be as low as the 100-ton 'Davy Crockett' projectile
of the '50s. The term 'tactical' as opposed to 'strategic' is
perhaps due to wishful thinking: if nuclear weapons are
part of overall strategy, the commitment to nuclear war is
irrevocable; but if the odd little weapon is used in large-
scale conventional war, one is not 'really' waging nuclear
war. The other side may not see it in this fashion.

And now we have the neutron bomb – 'enhanced
radiation/reduced blast' is the official term. With a typical
yield of a few kilotonnes, it is equivalent to low-yield
tactical fission weapons – whose effective military agent is
also prompt nuclear radiation, but whose large blast and
thermal radiation outputs lead to undesirable side-effects.
In the neutron bomb the nuclear radiation output is
enhanced. Consequently, for the same military effectiveness a much reduced total yield is feasible, leading to
significant reduction in the extent of thermal-radiation and
blast damage. Technically, the N-bomb approaches the
pure thermonuclear device – the most efficient nuclear
weapon conceivable. A 1-kiloton explosion could be
produced from the complete fusion of 6 grams apiece of D
and T; 56 grams of Pu-239 are needed to produce the same

(*Alexis Gilliland*)

effect by fission. 'Pure' fusion is also more deadly in that its emitted neutrons have nearly five times the energy of those from fission (average 14MeV from D-T fusion, 3MeV from fission). In terms of neutron energy output, a 20-kiloton fission bomb is no more deadly than a 1-kiloton D-T bomb.

But we are unable to eliminate the fissile trigger, so far; our technology has no other means of detonating a fusion device. Part of the explosive power of an N-bomb must come from the trigger; more of the neutrons will be absorbed in the bomb's own material. In terms of neutron output, a *practical* N-bomb could be as deadly at the same range as a standard weapon of five times the yield. Over most of the effective radius of the bomb, heat-flash and blast would be minimal while radiation reached fatal levels.

IV: The Receiving End

There is a need for widespread public understanding of the best informtion available on the effects of nuclear weapons.

US DEPARTMENT OF DEFENSE

A modern 1-megaton fusion bomb is exploded high in the air. What happens?

The energy of a million tons of exploding TNT is freed. The total fission-plus-fusion-plus-fission energy will be greater still, about 10% being 'delayed' nuclear radiation which will be emitted over a period of time by the fission products. 50% of the total energy goes into a blast-wave and 35% is emitted as thermal radiation; the last 5% consists of invisible neutrons and gamma-rays.

In the 1-megaton explosion the fireball can swell rapidly to approaching two kilometres across. Thermal radiation from this fireball can cause fairly severe burns on exposed skin at 20 kilometres distance on a clear day, while the flash of warmth can be felt at a distance six times greater. Heat rays are easily stopped by walls or even ordinary clothing if thick enough. More burns than expected were suffered at Hiroshima because of the fine, sunny weather; victims wore light and scanty clothing. Exposed flesh is directly at hazard, and thin garments which touch the skin are heated to produce indirect burns. In all, flash burns caused 20 to 30% of the Japanese deaths. The flash also starts fires, with their own normal hazards, and can damage the eye: there were many cases of temporary blindness, and permanent damage is possible. Sunny weather helps here, since in bright light the pupil is contracted to exclude radiation; there is also the ingrained instinct *not* to look at the Sun, which can apply to other sun-bright objects in the sky. Few Japanese eye injuries were noted, although later US experiments with megaton-range explosions at high altitude in darkness showed that burns on the retina were possible at 550 kilometres distance. The eye's adaptation to bright light would probably halve this distance.

Also released is a burst of gamma-rays and neutrons. These are less deadly than the explosive blast since for megaton-range weapons the zones of lethal radiation are still deadlier in terms of heat and blast, being so close to the actual fireball. A smaller weapon of 100 kilotons would produce lethal radiation at up to 1·5 kilometres, with many deaths and casualties in the next few hundred metres out. At these high levels the radiation – normally an insidious, unsensed killer – can be *felt*, as tingling or burning of the skin. In the lethal circle, symptoms appear within half an hour: the most strongly affected victims suffer damage to the central nervous system and go into tremors and convulsions; death comes in anything from one hour to two days. Less hard-hit victims suffer severe gastric disturbance (the intestines are very susceptible to massive radiation); death from circulatory collapse comes within two weeks. Casualties outside the surely-lethal zone suffer haemorrhages over a longer period, and may die from this or from infection in the next two months. Vomiting occurs in all these cases and in others less severe; loss of hair is frequent, and there is usually damage to the body's blood-renewing systems (which may be alleviated by bone-marrow transplant). Thus the effects of a 100-kiloton bomb; a 1-kiloton neutron bomb exploded at a few hundred metres would have similar effects, with the circle of quick death only slightly smaller – say a kilometre in radius – and severe radiation sickness at up to twice that distance, killing most victims in a month or so.

Radiation-shielding requires care. Gamma-rays are

stopped by a sufficient thickness of heavy material: steel and lead make fine shields. Against neutrons, however, they are less effective than light materials. There is a neat demonstration of this in neutron radiography – using neutrons one can photograph a plant, say, behind two inches of lead. (X-rays or gamma-rays might 'look' with difficulty through the lead, but to them the plant would be invisible.) This is because slower neutrons are more easily slowed further by collisions with elements of *low* atomic weight. A billiard ball cued at a large mass like the cushions will bounce off with energy almost unchanged, while a small mass like a ping-pong ball would be brushed aside. But a glancing blow on a ball of similar mass will share out the ball's original momentum, slowing it down. For neutrons, water is a good stopping material as hydrogen and oxygen have low masses. When sufficiently slowed, the neutrons can combine with hydrogen nuclei to form deuterium. This releases gamma-rays, so a neutron screen also needs heavier elements to block such rays. A few feet of concrete are adequate, especially when the proportion of heavy nuclei is increased by adding iron ore or barytes. This screen must surround the user totally for full protection; gamma-rays and neutrons are scattered in air and will 'shine' from directions other than that of the actual explosion.

Blast is a nuclear weapon's most destructive aspect: a simple shockwave like that of conventional explosives but of huge intensity. The 1-megaton bomb would destroy, through blast, practically every building within four kilometres of ground zero; a 1-kiloton neutron bomb would cause severe damage over a radius of only about 500 metres. These estimates ignore minor damage; the 1-megaton burst could break windows at 30 kilometres or more, but this is not considered to be of military importance – no matter what may be the feelings of people standing behind the windows.

At close range the pressure-waves harm people directly, damaging the eardrums and in severe cases the lungs. Indirect damage (e.g., from flying glass) was much more common at Hiroshima. There is the small consolation that blast travels relatively slowly; there is time to protect oneself between flash and blast. The shock from a 1-megaton explosion would be delayed by about 1·5 seconds at 1 kilometre, 20 seconds at 8 kilometres and nearly 40 seconds at 15 kilometres, giving time for people to adopt a safer position – near a stout wall and away from doors or windows if indoors, prone with head directly towards or away from the explosion if outdoors. Blast waves which cannot kill directly may still hurl one against walls or the ground – hence the prone position. For weapons of lower yield the blast takes still longer to arrive.

The final hazard of a nuclear weapon is fall-out – the radio-active wastes – which may be fused into the ground below the actual explosion, scattered across the country by local winds and carried around the world by high-altitude wind currents. Fall-out, although a great hazard of tests, will be a relatively minor danger of war: there are so many greater things to worry about. But, after twenty years, Bikini is still an unhealthy place to live in. Fall-out is the part of nuclear war which even the aggressors will regret: serving no military purpose, it has no place in this book, perhaps – except as another factor, one of the tiniest, which make those in power a little more reluctant to push the red nuclear buttons.

V: Fighting a Nuclear War

The NATO doctrine is that we will fight with conventional forces until we are losing, then we will fight with tactical nuclear weapons until we are losing, and then we will blow up the world.

MORTON HALPERIN,
former US Deputy Assistant Secretary of Defense

At Hiroshima 144,000 people were injured, nearly half fatally. It was not a large city; the population density was some 10,000 per square kilometre in the central zone where most deaths occurred. A modern supercity like London has several times this population density during the day, so that even a small 20-kiloton bomb could be expected to claim well over half a million victims. In practice, a nuclear device used in anger on London would be very much more powerful; strategists who consider such situations make their estimates in the convenient units of 'megadeaths', or millions of deaths.

But the situation is like that of nerve-gas delivery – frightful lethality mitigated by basic inefficiency. A 20-kiloton weapon killed 68,000 people at Hiroshima, which is reminiscent of those World War I figures of the thousands of bullets fired for each man killed. The allotment of an equivalent 0·3 tons of TNT to each member of the opposition seems more staggering than the power of the bomb itself. The energy of so much TNT is sufficient to lift a ten-ton weight more than 12 kilometres into the air to be dropped on each hapless victim. The reader will rightly suspect that this is not precisely what is meant by 'overkill' . . . But this approach is biased towards individual human lives, ignoring other effects of a nuclear strike – square kilometres of smashed buildings, megacasualties to complement the megadeaths. What is destroyed is a city (or military installation): one bomb, one city. Overkill means having more than one bomb per target, as a precaution against failure of the first strike or strikes.

When and where will the strike be made? A common view is that nuclear war is unthinkable – but, if it happens, it will be all-out war. The ICBMs (InterContinental Ballistic Missiles) will rise from their silos and roar up beyond the atmosphere, while smaller missiles like Polaris will be launched from submarines; flights of bombers take off, laden with more nuclear weapons which will not arrie until well after the first strike missiles. Some or most, of the CCBMs, will be MIRV (Multiple Independently Retargetable Vehicles) carriers which split upon re-entry to release a sheaf of smaller missiles, spreading out to confuse the defences. By now the whole sky is filled with falling objects, most of them decoys and debris; below, radar screens display blizzards. Interceptors rise, radar-guided to the most likely incoming objects (the biggest and the fastest). A typical interceptor is a low-yield weapon in its own right, intended to 'kill' the interlopers above their own detonation altitude. Small fireballs bloom in space or in the thin upper air, where blastwaves blow the falling debris about the sky, exposing the identities of the heavier incoming missiles. At closer range this blast can disable enemy bombs; the thermal and gamma flash can burn off the outer layers of the re-entry vehicle so rapidly as to deliver an explosive hammerblow; a flood of neutrons, penetrating the warhead's casing may heat the fissile material and thus cause damage. Relatively slight changes in the imploding system can reduce or even eliminate the nuclear yield. But there may not be many interceptors; their use is limited by treaty, and it's known that current strike capabilities could saturate an ABM (Anti-Ballistic Missile) system.

Some of the incoming missiles may be equipped for evasive action, changing course to confuse the interceptors; they slip down to their appropriate altitude (calculated for maximum devastation of the target below) and explode. Precise timing and placing is essential, for such explosions can knock out 'friendly' missiles more effectively than mere interceptors. These unwieldy weapons *are* capable of precision: the US Minuteman III ICBM is said to be accurate to within about 300 metres of its target, and the USSR SS-18 and SS-19 have similar performance. Accuracy of targeting cuts two ways; the defenders know missiles should be deployed for maximum effect and can thus judge the probable courses of weapons meant for various targets: interceptors will be ready to strike up along these lines . . .

The first wave of attack is over; the missiles are radioactive wrecks or nodding mushroom clouds. The bombers throb slowly across the North Pole, carrying SRAMs (Short-Range Attack Missiles) with a range of 150 kilometres or more. The antagonists assess the effects of the first exchange: how many missiles do they have left? Where? How many cities do *we* have left? Which of us has suffered more? Is one of us winning? In practice, a first strike made by the US against the USSR or *vice versa* could eliminate virtually all the victim's ICBM silos. 'Second-strike capability' is mainly provided by SLBMs (Submarine-Launched Ballistic Missiles) and the bombers, although work is afoot on underground tunnel silos kilometres in length, in which the actual position of an ICBM would be unknown. It takes a ground-level hit to destroy ICBMs in hardened silos, so one defence involves forests of steel rods to impale missiles just before impact! Also suggested are high-velocity gasguns and underground nuclear detonations which fling debris up at the incoming missiles.

In such a nuclear Armageddon, thousands of warheads would be delivered. Even at this deadly level there are distinctions. Kahn has suggested as 'escalation ladder' of 44 rungs as a guide to nuclear warfare; although outdated in part it remains interesting and provocative. The lowest rung is 'ostensible crisis'; nuclear war becomes conceivable at Rung 10; actual nuclear war begins at Rung 21; the battle just described could be as low as Rung 36 (an attempt to destroy enemy forces while avoiding civilian targets; i.e., sparing missile installations near cities) or as high as Rung 44, 'spasm or insensate war', where everything is flung into a final orgy of destruction. Immediate casualties are likely to level off well before total depopulation, even so – missiles will not be targeted on thinly populated areas. Fall-out is another matter. A US strike against the USSR with 1000 weapons could at once kill 40% of the population; quadrupling the attack brings the immediate deaths to about 50%. The ultimate death tolls would be far larger – estimated at about 70% in the first case, 90% in the second. The effects of a USSR strike on the US would be comparable.

War at this level is unlikely without severe provocation. Kahn does not insist that every rung of his ladder must be climbed as disagreement escalates to nuclear war – but, in the absence of actual insanity afflicting an entire government, it should be safe to assume that the dreaded Rung 39, at which nuclear targeting on cities begins, will not be reached without pausing at lower states of crisis. At each level it's still possible to turn back. Here nuclear war differs fundamentally from past warfare, in that it's far less likely that everything will be thrown into the battle. Total war now means rapid elimination of both sides; a controlled war of restraint, bluff and limited nuclear use is more likely. Nuclear escalation results from threats and counter-threats in which one country or alliance tries to coerce another without provoking full-scale war. (At present, the usual form of coercion is low-level conventional or guerilla aggression.) Kahn's metaphor for this is the game 'chicken', whose two players drive cars in a collision course; the first to swerve away from destruction is the loser. Nuclear diplomacy likewise intimidates the opposition into backing down for fear of the outcome; it might be cynically added that statesmen are more concerned over nuclear than conventional war, since now there is no question of 'sending the boys off to fight' – when H-bombs fall, even statesmen are at risk. But, despite such influences towards caution, it's an unpleasant fact that victory in 'chicken' and perhaps in nuclear escalation can go to the side which is prepared to take more risks.

A strategy for 'chicken' is to be conspicuously drunk on starting, to wear almost opaque sunglasses to show lack of judgement, and to toss the steering-wheel out of the window once the car is set on its collision course. The other driver might then lose his nerve and back down – unless he, too, is trying the same strategy. A government which can sound totally irrational – indeed, psychopathic – has a sort of advantage over one concerned for peace. Fortunately, nuclear diplomacy is more complex than 'chicken'; an apparently irrational government could frighten other countries into a 'pre-emptive strike' on the principle of attack being the best form of defence (not necessarily true in nuclear war). This 'rational' response to an irrational threat could lead to an unrestrained nuclear conflict, since the full nuclear delivery capability of a country is virtually impossible to neutralise. Such considerations as this could make nuclear politics akin to playing 'chicken' on a cliff road, where the choice is to sacrifice oneself for the irrational player or to die with him . . . Imagine an Adolf Hitler with a nuclear arsenal.

The notion of an escalation ladder rooted in mere

disagreement and ascending its neatly tabulated rungs to all-out war is perhaps dangerous. The opposition may draw the dividing lines in different places. In a 'controlled' nuclear war one might apply pressure by shifting from Rung 37, with nuclear strikes on military installations, to Rung 38, which is the same without avoiding civilian populations. In Kahn's 1965 assessment, the difference between these rungs is much less than that before the next series, 39 upwards, in which cities become targets in their own right. An enemy might not see it in the same way. An enemy, indeed, might panic and at the first use of nuclear weapons *in any form* rush to Rung 39, where a slow-motion war is fought, trading city for city. Or higher still.

For where does nuclear use begin? Around 7000 tactical nuclear weapons have been deployed in Europe's NATO forces; they are intended to supplement conventional forces in the event of everwhelming attack from Warsaw Pact countries. A tactical weapon is a little thing, hardly worth mentioning, only about as potent as the Hiroshima bomb . . . These are the 'mini-nukes'; the scale runs further down to 'micro-nukes', which can be launched from hand-held bazookas. Neutron bombs would weigh in at a kiloton or less. These weapons are being rivalled from below by advanced conventional weapons of great power, but it is still clear that the nuclear threshold – the point at which one starts using nuclear weapons – is the most important of present-day warfare. The investment in tactical nukes is symptomatic of the old human desire to put one's cake simultaneously into mouth and pocket – to take advantage of the concentrated destructive power of nuclear weapons without precipitating full-scale nuclear war. This is not a sound approach. At present, the common assumption is that nuclear warfare of any kind represents so high a level of escalation as to threaten world-wide holocaust. To replace this healthy fear with some official or unofficial limit on kilotonnage of tactical weapons would remove that first colossal leap into the unthinkable. To shift metaphors, it could become too like C. S. Lewis's gradual road to Hell: '. . . the gentle slope, soft underfoot, without sudden turnings, without milestones, without signposts . . .'

Meanwhile, a nuclear stalemate prevails, since the super-powers recognise the balance defined in the Mutual Assured Destruction (MAD) policy – no matter who starts the war, both antagonists can be wiped out. Therefore, no sane government will start a nuclear war. The amount of cheer afforded by this axiom depends on one's opinion of the governments concerned. Certainly they might have chosen a happier acronym.

CHAPTER THREE

THE EDGE OF SCIENCE FICTION

I: Towards a Death Ray

And at that fateful signal, his countless ships and planetary installations discharged the full, awesome power of their primary projectors, the blazing beams of destruction combining into a hellish flare of incalculable incandescence before which no defence might prevail!

Nivek snarled in rage. 'Missed!'

MAC MALSENN, *Sex Pirates of the Blood Asteroid*

There is a game which scientists play, called 'Well, *would* it work?' – the object of attention being some standard gimmick of science fiction. It is usually played light-heartedly, to the relief of the writers themselves, who mostly do not claim to offer detailed sociological and technological blueprints of the future. Just as writers pick interesting people to write about, so they choose interesting – not always probable – future settings. They have an equivocal record as prophets, correct 'predictions' generally being produced by accident amid a much larger output of incorrect ones. As for the scientists – it was Arthur C. Clarke who formulated the rule that when a distinguished scientist announces that something is impossible, its future success is at once ensured. Such false predictions often arise through the use of an inapplicable theory: bumble-bees 'can't possibly fly' because aerodynamic formulae don't happen to allow for their flexible wings,* and space travel is

---

*Virgil wrote that bees in flight carried tiny stones lest they be blown away. Bee-power has declined since those days.

impossible because one would have to carry an absurd amount of fuel (solution: the multistage rocket). My favourite example of this from a spoof SF story runs: 'It was well known that spaceflight was impossible owing to the impenetrability of the crystal spheres in which the planets were embedded.'

And one of the favourite 'impossibilities' of SF was the ray-gun, imported to Earth by H. G. Wells's heat-ray-wielding Martians and used increasingly ever since. The standard argument against this was that, for such a device to work, it was necessary for some part of it to be hotter than the target. The Sun, the light-bulb filament and the electric fire are all hotter than most of the things they irradiate; a weapon which could vaporise metal at a distance would need to be so very hot that it would also vaporise itself and probably its owner. This theory may have encouraged some writers' diversification into guns with unlikely calibres (firing tiny bullets wose effective range would be only a few metres, or massive ones whose recoil would hurl the user to the ground), but 'energy-beams' generally remained popular. One knew it to be a special form of energy, since the beams could be seen as searing white (red, violet, etc.) lines through space despite the lack of air to scatter radiation sideways and make the beam visible.

Then, in 1958, the laser was suggested as a theoretical possibility. There already existed a form a low-power microwave amplifier called the maser, which stood for Molecular Amplification by Stimulated Emission of Radiation. It was used in radar receivers. The laser was first termed an 'optical maser', and later 'light' was substituted for 'molecular' to give the more familiar acronym.

In the previous chapter, atomic electrons were ignored as having very much less potential for energy-release than the nucleus. In the physics of light, electrons are all-important and energies are never so high as to shake the nucleus. This does not mean that electronic and chemical effects are always negligible when compared with those of the nucleus: a candle generates more heat than a fragment of plutonium, the former having low-energy reactions (combustion) going on at a great rate while the latter's high-energy reactions (nuclear decay) are relatively infrequent. We are presently concerned not with chemical effects but with the interaction of radiation – light in particular – with an atom's orbiting electrons. The solar-system model of the atom provides a picture of what an electron effectively does – it orbits the nucleus, prevented from escaping by electromagnetic attraction and prevented from falling inwards by its own motion (i.e., 'centrifugal force'). Now if a lightwave – a photon – hits the electron and gives it more energy, it will go faster and pull further from the nucleus; as it moves outward the electromagnetic pull slows it until it stabilises in a wider orbit. Conversely, if the electron were now to emit a photon of the same energy as the one just absorbed, it would sink again to the tighter orbit. This model of light absorption and emission has something wrong with it, though, for just any photon will not do: only certain energies, certain wavelengths of light, can be absorbed to kick the atom into its higher or excited state.

The effect can be explained in terms of the quantum theory, which takes into account the electron's dubious state – in some ways a definite particle, in others more like a wave-motion. But physicists accepted the way atoms behave before developing this theory, and for the sake of simplicity and sanity so shall we. To summarise a very long series of observations and deductions, it turns out that – while in the solar-system model any orbital distance from the nucleus is possible – in reality only a certain number of states or 'energy levels' is permitted. Electrons *cannot exist* in an atom at one of these fixed energy levels. The permitted energies of photons which can be absorbed are those which lift an electron exactly from its level to a higher one; conversely, photons can only be emitted with energies corresponding to the difference between a higher and lower level. An atom is very precisely tuned. The general layout of the electronic energy levels is such that transitions from one to another involve the absorption or emission of photons of infrared radiation, or visible light, or ultraviolet, or, at the highest energies, X-rays. (Gamma-rays come from transitions between *nuclear* energy levels.) Microwave energies are also possible in the least energetic transitions. The characteristic orange of a sodium lamp comes from a particularly favoured transition in the sodium atom.

Having defined emission and absorption, we can define stimulated emission. An electron in an excited state – at a higher level than its normal one – does not necessarily rush straight down again by emitting its photon: the state can be 'quasi-stable'. However, if the atom is bathed in radiation of the frequency corresponding to that of the photon it is currently not emitting, it can be stimulated into emission, as a bell resonates when its note is struck on the piano. It turns out that the stimulated radiation is emitted in the same direction (as well as the same frequency, polarisation and phase) as that which has stimulated it – one photon, in other words, has become two. Those two can encounter more excited atoms to become four, and eight, and sixteen, and thirty-two . . . it is an optical chain reaction.

There are, of course, difficulties. Large numbers of stimulated emissions are possible only when there is a 'population inversion' – when in a collection of similar atoms the electrons in the higher (excited) energy-level are more numerous than those in the lower. In practice, devious and indirect means of achieving this state are used, 'pumping' electrons about a whole series of energy-levels in order to build up the population of the level from which emission can be stimulated. It is important to choose atoms or molecules which offer suitable patterns of energy-levels. This gives us the material for the light amplifier, which can either work in a sudden pulse, draining all the stored energy of the higher level as in the first laser experiments, or by a more complex mechanism whereby a separate route of energy-levels is used to replenish constantly the electron-population of the vital one. This light amplifier is something like a subcritical mass of plutonium, which will produce a shower of neutrons (photons) from an initial one; the shower then escapes and all is over. The true laser has a mirror at each end of a tube of 'lasing' material (an inevitable coinage), so that the surge of photons flares up and down the tube, growing more and more intense until the saturation point when all the excited atoms have been stimulated to emit a photon (pulsed laser) or when they are being stimulated as fast as they become excited (continuous-wave laser). Any odd photons which do not travel along the axis of the tube will lead to small off-axis bursts which rapidly leave the laser through its sides – so that by a process of 'natural selection' an almost perfectly parallel beam of light is maintained (fig. 3). Finally, the mirrors are carefully adjusted so that the space between them is an exact number of wavelengths of the light; for the first ruby laser the wavelength was 6943Å or 0·00006943 cm – a fine adjustment indeed. Then the wave-trains going up and down the tube will overlap in perfect phase, producing a standing wave as though the tube were an organ pipe – a resonating beam of light. If one of the mirrors is partly transparent, much of this light can be allowed to escape in a narrow beam: the rest remains to keep up the oscillations in the tube.

This emitted beam can be very intense indeed. A typical small ruby laser is activated by a millisecond flashgun using

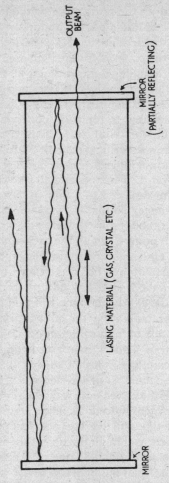

Fig. 3 'Natural selection' in a simple laser: the unwanted off-axis rays bounce from mirror to mirror until they leave the system, while rays along the axis reinforce themselves, overlapping again and again.

1000 joules of electrical energy (one megawatt for one millisecond). The light output is a mere 3J of radiation at 6943Å (red light) – an efficiency of 0·3%. (For comparison, an ordinary light-bulb has an efficiency of about 8% and a flourescent tube of about 26%.) the beam is 0·5 cm across and can be made so nearly paralled as to spread no more than to a three-kilometre-diameter spot when beamed the 400,000 kilometres to the Moon. The first weapon possibilities become apparent when the beam is focused to a small spot with a diameter of a few wavelengths. Power densities of something like one million watts per square centimetre are reached; the local heating is sufficient to drill a hole through a steel ruler.

All sorts of materials can be used for lasers. The first one was a pulsed ruby laser demonstrated in 1960, which was followed by a continuous-wave helium-neon gas laser. Low-power solid-state lasers were also developed, pumped by direct injection of electric current across a semi-conductor junction. Laser action as been produced in liquids, and in compounds of fissile materials such as gaseous UF_6 pumped directly from a reactor's neutron output 'Pumping' is a catchall term describing any effective method of getting energy into a laser system; more recent high-power systems like the CO_2 gas-dynamic laser convert heat energy at high efficiency (5%), with the required energy states being generated in a gas-flow expanding at supersonic speeds. The chemical laser converts reaction energy; hydrogen and fluorine become HF (hydrofluoric acid) and produce much energy, the result being highly-excited HF molecules which form the lasing mixture.

We can now look again at the argument for the laser's impossibility. The false assumption made that a 'deathray' would require a source which emitted energy by the thermal-radiation laws, whereby emission takes place in all directions (owing to the random, statistical nature of thermal processes) and the average beam intensity falls off as the square of the distance. A laser is a highly directional device which, even without a focussing lens, concentrates its output energy into a tightly controlled beam. The lasing medium *is* heated, but not to the exorbitant levels suggested by a theory which insists that the material must radiate through its sheer heat, like a light-bulb filament. J. B. S. Haldane observed in 1939 – quite correctly, from the viewpoint of contemporary science – 'A simple calculation shows that any substance hot enough to send out such a ray would not merely melt, but explode into fiery gas in a tiny fraction of a second.'

Of course there is a large difference between having a laser and having a workable laser weapon. It took many years to travel from a theory of nuclear reactions and mass-energy equivalence to an actual nuclear weapon, though nuclear reactions are vastly more energetic. Lasers began as an interesting demonstration of the 1958 theory, and for some time afterwards were characterised as 'a brilliant solution in search of a problem'. They provide a source of coherent light at a fixed frequency, and are thus helpful in the optics laboratory (there is a celebrated experiment in which students are provided with a laser and a metre rule and asked to measure the wavelength of the light!). A laser beam defines what is virtually a perfect straight line, and thus has applications in surveying work. Pulsed lasers can deliver tiny, precise bursts of heat for surgery like the rewelding of detached retinas. The tight beam means that laser light can be bounced off the Moon (especially when Apollo astronauts left mirrors up there), and used to measure rather precisely the changing distance from Earth to Moon. Precision laser 'measurement' at short ranges permits detection of movements as small as the vibrations caused in a window by the sound waves from a conversation in the room within – hence a surveillance device which interprets these movements at a distance and converts them back to sound. Further exploration of laser-measurement possibilities produced the first weapons applications, in the form of laser range-finders, gunsight alignment aids and bomb or missile guidance systems.

But although enterprising science-fiction writers have been industriously filing the serial numbers off their old death-rays and relabelling them as lasers, the hand-held laser weapon remains unlikely. Steel companies now use 10-kilowatt lasers capable of cutting through an inch of steel at a great rate, but such systems and their power supplies are just too big for handguns. It has been said that a laser big enough to be a real war weapon would be so big that it would not *need* to work: you simply drop it on the enemy. Certainly no one is presently considering a laser hand-weapon as a realistic possibility (it may not be possible even in theory); laser artillery is the objective of present-day research. High-power continuous-wave CO_6 lasers have attained output powers in excess of half a megawatt in the infrared spectrum; this may be enough for an offensive weapon, although probably still higher power-levels must be reached. Certainly, after travelling so far from the 1-milliwatt output power of the original continuous-wave gas lasers (fearful weapons which at close range can actually damage the eyes of anyone so careless as to look directly along the beam into the lasing cavity), a further power increase by factors of 100 or more seems not unreasonable.

Why trouble? Why use lasers and what good will they do? Firstly, of course, there is the overwhelming argument that if research is not kept up an enemy may find laser applications deadlier by far than those known today. This attitude may err on the side of paranoia, but only when effective laser weapons have been either developed or *proved* unworkable can a government feel quite secure. Laser artillery is also attractive, odd though it may sound, through the concept's sheer elegance. It is the ultimate refinement of all the crude weapons discussed in Chapter 1: a device which delivers destructive energy, *and nothing else*, to the target. Because nothing material is hurled at the enemy, it is possible to present the appearance of an infinite firing capacity; one cannot run out of physical ammunition, and can draw on the resources of a country (e.g., *via* electrical networks) to carry on firing. Also effectively infinite is the delivery speed. Photons travelling at the speed of light (they can go no slower) are the quickest possible way of delivering energy to a target; for example, imagine a missile at a height of 10 kilometres, travelling at 10,000 kph. A ground-based laser fires at it; in the time taken for the beam to travel up through the atmosphere, the missile will have moved on – by a little under ten centimetres. Moreover, sufficiently sophisticated equipment can track the beam very rapidly across the sky by deflecting it with some form of mirror. (One of the little problems which have yet to be solved is the production of mirrors which will withstand this treatment. High reflectivity is required, and improved systems of cooling immediately behind the reflecting surface; this is a matter of engineering and should be sorted out before long.) The problems of ballistics can be forgotten; here is a weapon which 'travels' in a straight line to its target, so quickly that there is no need for predictions of where the target will be in future – you fire at what you see, or what the radar shows.

The actual 'kill mechanism' by which the laser disables its target will depend on the target's vulnerability. If sufficient power can be delivered, the target will quite simply be vaporised by deposited heat. This is an extreme case, and in general such measures should be unnecessary. A manned spacecraft or high-altitude plane could be disabled simply by melting or vaporising a hole in it to let out the air; vehicles with fuel tanks or (like missiles) payloads of explosive could be blown up by well-placed bursts of heat. High energy-depositions also lead to shockwaves (produced by reaction force as material boils off like a jet) and X-ray production from the multiply excited atoms of the target; both can cause havoc, especially to electronics. Less dramatically, slower heating leads to a possible use as an incendiary weapon – perhaps to be used from satellites against cities.

Lasers could be especially powerful weapons against satellites, which travel relatively slowly from the viewpoint of a ground station and have little chance to cool down during attack (no cooling air currents, and an object must become quite hot before it cools effectively by emission of radiant heat). The electronic communications apparatus of a satellite is particularly vulnerable, electronics being sensitive to heating; without communications a satellite is often useless. Moreover, still lower levels of power will be enough to incapacitate reconnaissance satellites and other devices such as optically or radar-guided missiles, simply by dazzling them; intense laser radiation can temporarily overload electronic and optical sensors without necessarily destroying them. There have been US claims that just this has been attempted against their satellites from ground-based USSR lasers.

This brief look at the possibilities makes it sound as if the problems have really been solved – if lasers can cut up steel plates at hundreds of centimetres per minute (and that as an effective commercial proposition, no mere laboratory demonstration), it's surely just a question of pointing one of these steelworks lasers into the air? Unfortunately *the air* is one of the greatest problems. Those steel-cutting lasers work effectively at ranges measured in centimetres, but to be of use as weapons they must force their energy through kilometres of atmosphere. The high-power lasers generally produce infrared radiation (of lower frequency than red, the lowest-frequency visible light), and unfortunately air contains some very enthusiastic absorbers of infrared – CO_2 and water vapour in particular – so that atmospheric lasers are restricted to the wavelengths where such absorption is the least. Energy is also lost to the air *via* electrical breakdowns – since beams of electromagnetic radiation actually consist of flickering electric and magnetic fields, and if the radiation is very intense and coherent the fields may tear electrons loose from atoms (ionisation). The energy used to do this is wasted. This also means that, although IR beams are theoretically invisible, a high-intensity beam in air shows as a 'dotted line' of sparks produced by ionisation breakdowns. A third problem is that air is an optical material in its own right, having a refractive index greater than that of vacuum – if a lens of air were suspended somehow in vacuum, it would focus light (although very weakly). This would not matter if the air's refractive index were constant; but it varies with density. Winds, atmospheric turbulence and the thinning of height all involve density changes which produce 'beam wander', diverting the laser beam just as light is bent through flawed glass. Since the air also becomes heated and thus alters in refractive index along the actual beam path, there is a further lens effect which throws the beam out of focus ('thermal bloom'). The beam is also scattered, becoming broader and less intense as a result of diffraction by small particles in the atmosphere. Almost it seems that the foe could ask for no better shield against laser fire than a few kilometres of thin air.

And yet even so, a test under ideal conditions has shown that a large atmospheric laser *can* destroy a small anti-tank missile at 1 kilometre range. It's a start.

There are several lesser problems. Military lasers will

have to be rugged and reliable (nuclear weapons would need to be much tougher were they used more than once), and capable of going into operation very swiftly – ICBMs move quickly, and a laser defence against such missiles must handle a fair number in a short period of time. If laser artillery ever moves on to the battlefield, even greater ruggedness will be expected, and their actual operation must be made simple and foolproof. On the battlefield there are also difficulties of power supply: electric gas-discharge lasers imply large generators or easily cut wires, and the HF laser has an *extremely* toxic exhaust of hydrofluoric gas, so that the CO_2 gas-dynamic laser now seems the most plausible. All three are expensive units with costs in the millions. A cost-sensitive military organisation will not use lasers at such prices unless they can either do a better job than anything cheaper, or do something which no other weapon can achieve. Certainly a battlefield laser will not be built for use on people – indeed, a battlefield laser seems the least likely of possible laser weapons. Something *that* expensive is far safer behind the lines . . . where there is a need for the most effective use of ground-based lasers, as a ballistic missile defence. Considerable development must be made before even this is feasible – far more likely is the prospect of satellite-mounted lasers, which, firing through space at their targets, would avoid the many major problems which afflict atmospheric lasers (as discussed above). Further notes on such weapons will be found in Chapter 4; meanwhile we can consider how things may be protected against laser fire.

The most effective defence, at first glance, is the simplest. If the target is a perfect mirror, the beam should simply bounce off harmlessly. However, a perfect mirror is one of those engineer's dreams (like frictionless bearings or 100% efficient power-sources) which cannot in practice be made. And if the surface is not *perfectly* reflective, a sufficiently high beam power will eventually break it down – as will happen to the eflector mirrors of the laser itself, which presumably must be frequently replaced. One can imagine a 'double-barrelled' laser combining a super-high-power pulsed laser with a more sedate continuous-wave model: the first emits a pulse lasting for less than a nanosecond at incredible intensity, which degrades the mirror surface enough for the continuous-wave laser to get a toehold (so to speak) and finish the job over the next second or so. The mirror-surface over the rest of the target can then become a disadvantage for a satellite, since it prevents cooling. (A perfect 'black body' absorbs and emits the absolute maximum of radiation for its temperature; a perfect 'white body' or mirror absorbs nothing – i.e., reflects everything – and emits nothing.) Indeed it may be that a satellite cannot be protected by mirror-plating; its own trapped heat from battery or solar-cell use could rise to the point where the electronics failed.

A mirror-surface would also be very vulnerable to other damage from conventional weapons, even minimal damage such as scratches, dents, scrapes, discolorations – the mirror could be made quite useless with nothing more lethal than an aerosol-bomb of black paint! And of course a bright, reflecting object is the perfect target for an optical seeker missile. There are, however, other effects which may provide protection against laser attack: for example, the puff of ionised gas emitted owing to the first heating of the target can absorb quantities of laser energy. Under certain conditions the gas forms a wave which travels along the attacking beam, absorbing and scattering it at a furious rate, and thus providing considerable protection. The notion of such an automatic defence triggered by the laser itself is elegant but possibly far-fetched – no one is sure whether the effect will work when the target is a missile travelling at high speed, and almost certainly it will not work in vacuum. And, of course, various means of piercing such a defence are under consideration. The beam strength of the laser could be made to fluctuate so that the puff of absorbing gas disappears before the next burst of radiation; or the beam could be moved across the target surface, melting it without using such intensityas to generate the 'absorption wave.'

For space, more fanciful defences have been suggested, such as clouds of metallic particles (e.g., aluminium dust) which would absorb and scatter the beam in this same fashion . . . but even if released rapidly and automatically upon detection of a laser strike, it's unlikely that such a screen could be formed in the fraction of a second available. Besides, if the target ship is accelerating it will rapidly leave its protective cloud behind.

To summarize, lasers as weapons in their own right seem highly promising as space-based missile defences, and not implausible as ground-based ones. Laser artillery on a terrestrial battlefield is less likely, and laser hand-weapons less likely still. It is the highly destructive 'death-ray' applications which are implausible on a battlefield – much more feasible would be a lower-power dazzler or blinder. It is possible, as noted previously, to damage the retina permanently by looking into the beam of a tiny laboratory-model milliwatt laser; a logical though unpleasant extension of this is a high-powered laser which by means of servo-operated mirrors sends its beams sweeping and flashing rapidly over a possibly hostile landscape. Anyone looking towards it is blinded, permanently if the power is high enough. Periscopes, gunsights, binoculars and optical instruments in general would transmit the blinding energy to the user's eye – concentrated by the lenses, if any. It took thousands of men with rifles to keep the enemy's head down in World War I; one blinder could police a whole landscape. Of course protective goggles could be worn, ones which did not transmit light at the laser frequency; to get around this, the frequency could be changed at irregular intervals. One would need a TV-aimed gun to put the blinder out of action; probably the laser would be unharmed, only its mirror-system being exposed. A less potent version of this is said to have been used by US planes over Vietnam, which swept the land below with a low-intensity beam; no harm was done to the naked eye, but observers incautious enough to use binoculars found that the concentrated beam fried their retinas.

The ability of the pulsed laser to deliver a tremendous amount of energy in a very short time has led to much consideration of its use to touch off a fusion reaction. If one takes a pellet of frozen deuterium (or D-T mixture, or perhaps a plastic with D or T substitute for its hydrogen) and blasts it with intense laser radiation from every side, the pellet surface boils away and expands in a blast of gas. The reaction forces add to radiation pressure to compress the pellet, and if things go right the result is a super-compressed fragment of extremely hot material, so hot and dense that the nuclei are driven together with sufficient energy for fussion. This is still a promising line of research for fusion power, although so far it has not been possible to extract more energy than is put in. Also there are vast engineering problems – how to pulse the multiple laser system hundreds of times per second, how to feed fresh fuel-pellets to the right place at the right time, and so on. At the time of writing the world's biggest laser system is the 20-beam US Shiva installation, which on its first attempt produced several thousand million fusions in a D-T pellet, thus releasing fusion energy equal to almost 0·0007% of that used to drive the laser . . . The reason for mentioning all this peacetime activity is that there have been one or two weak suggestions that laser compression could lead to a clean fusion bomb; with a laser pulse substituting for the standard fissile trigger, the energy release from the imploded pellet would be a pure fusion explosion. Unfortunately the idea is presently unpromising owing to the sheer size of the lasers needed – the Shiva laser has amplifier chains hundreds of metres in length – and the huge cost, many times greater than that of the prospective laser weapons already mentioned. Moreover, even the improved Shiva Nova fusion research laser installation is not intended to implode pellets more than a few millimetres across (and so far it's failed to meet expectations when performing this, it's intended task) . . . For the foreseeable future, a laser-compressed fusion bomb is not practical: absurdly bulky and expensive, with such low yield as to be virtually harmless. It would be more effective to point the lasers themselves at the enemy, despite the disadvantages already outlined.

II: Impure Energies

Consider this: A helium-filled balloon that floats upon the top of the atmosphere; below it is slung the gondola in which the navigation computers, communications gear, fuel tanks and so forth are housed. To the rear of the gondola are attached rocket thrusters; at its front sits the control cabin, in which a crew of pressure-suited patriots are ensconced. Below the gondola is slung the mouth of the tube that leads back to the ground station, wherein the proton accelerator sits ready to spew forth its lethal particles. In times of peace, then, the balloon floats serenely in space, maintaining its position by computer-controlled thrust bursts, whose frequency is keyed to data transmitted from selected comsats; crews are ferried up to the gondola for periods of duty by the appropriate space

> *shuttles. When the ICBMs loom upon the horizon,*
> *however, the gondola casts loose from the baloon,*
> *deploys its wings, fires its thrusters and, dragging tte*
> *mouth of the tube with it, heads for the incoming*
> *enemy missile. Once in position, the now-ready*
> *proton accelerator fires, the missile is destroyed,*
> *and the crew become Heroes of the Soviet Union. Or*
> *dead. Mainly dead . . .*
>
> JOSEPH M. NICHOLAS

The more engineering-minded science-fiction writers had one or two alternative death-ray designs which were intended to sound more plausible than the 'impossible' heat ray. For example, Arthur C. Clarke (in *Earthlight*) offered a jet of molten metal magnetically accelerated to tremendous speed, which may be squirted destructively through space. This is base materialism and has no place in a chapter devoted mainly to energy-weapons: in any case, it doesn't sound particularly efficient (why not accelerate a solid missile?) and may well have been an excuse for having, just for once, a 'beam' which really *could* theoretically be seen as 'a solid bar of light stabbing at the stars' . . . But something very close to a pure-energy weapon is a particle-accelerator emitting fast electrons or protons: the term *particle* is used to describe electrons, protons, neutrons and the rest, although all (and especially the electron) are made fuzzy by Heisenbergian uncertainty: they are simultaneously particles, with the solid compactness that term implies, and wave-motions, to be described only in quantum mechanics. Without delving deeply into such murky questions, we know that beams of fast particles can convey large amounts of destructive energy, and are in theory much simpler to produce than the laser beam.

Electron beams are the simplest of all. Many substances, when heated, emit electrons which are 'boiled off' at their surfaces: this is the purpose of the heaters which gave old radio valves their nostalgic glow. In a simple diode valve, there are two metal plates called the cathode, which emits electrons, and the anode: connect a battery between them, with the positive leads going to the anode, and the emitted electrons will accelerate through the electric field which now exists between the plates – and a current flows. (The point of the term 'valve' is that it won't flow with the battery connected the other way round – the anode doesn't emit electrons.) In its journey each electron is acceleratedto an energy of 1eV for each volt of potential difference between the plates; with a high voltage and a hole in the anode to let some of these fast electrons slip through, the result is a beam of electrons. Such a beam is swept about in a TV tube, to form an image as the electrons strike light from phosphors on the tube face.

Perhaps the first thoughts of a beam weapon came to someone who left an oscilloscope turned on too brightly. The tube in an oscilloscope is used to display pictures of electric waveforms (often more aesthetically gratifying than TV . . . but I digress); with no imput it may simply show a bright spot, and if it's made too bright the beam will burn off the phosphor in that region, or even punch a hole clean through the tube window – and this with electron energies of only a few hundred eV. The effect is produced by simple heating. Unfortunately such electron-beams have a range in air which can be measured in metres. Higher voltages produce faster and more expensive electrons with longer ranges – a few hundred kilovolts gives electrons of much higher energy (hundreds of keV, naturally) which, on striking metal targets, produce tremendous heat and high-energy radiation in the form of X-rays. Such a beam could obviously damage electronics and even metal in time (X-ray targets have to be made of the hardest metals and artificially cooled). Again, however, the range is not all that great – indeed, an X-ray tube will not work unless evacuated (although this is also necessary to prevent the hot cathode and target from burning away, as an electric-light filament burns up when the glass bulb is cracked). Very soon we reach the stage where higher voltages cannot be provided – potentials in the megavolts are hard to maintain, since they flash to earth at the slightest provocation, breaking down air and insulation in a shower of miniature lightning bolts. It is possible to make electron accelerators which push the electrons 'a little at a time' without requiring massive voltages; linear accelerators (linacs) do this, as the name implies, along a straight line and can produce electron energies of hundreds of MeV, while machines like the betatron and synchrotron trap them in a circle and give them a push each time they pass GO, so to speak, until energies in the GeV or 1000 MeV range are reached. This sounds deadly enough – but only very low current outputs can be obtained from these machines, and there aren't *enough* electrons to do significant damage. Worse still, the initial advantages of the electron – its electric charge and low mass, making it easy to accelerate – now become drawbacks. Electrons repel each other, and if a reasonable number are being squirted from a beam device the repulsion throws the beam out of focus with great rapidity. With this problem taken into consideration, even a space-based e-beam weapon (without the difficulties of atmosphere) seems dificult indeed. Other problems were considered by George O. Smith in a story called 'Recoil', where after a few firings his space-station's electron beam weapon refuses to work – such a vast positive charge (through loss of electrons) had built up that electrostatic attraction effectively prevented further shots from leaving the gun.

Abandoning electronics for the moment, let's consider other particles for beam weapons. the muon or 'heavy electron' is less prone to beam-spread owing to its greater mass – however, it is unstable with a half-life of microseconds and can be produced only by a moderately complex series of nuclear reactions which cannot be performed in sufficient numbers to provide a killing beam current. It seems that we must move to the really heavy particles: nucleons. The neutron is a non-starter – literally – since there is no way to accelerate an uncharged particle. The proton (hydrogen nucleus), despite being a massive and damaging particle, has its own problems. Proton beams are classified as non-penetrating radiation; their effective range in air is very short since protons have an irresistible compulsion to pick up electrons and form neutral hydrogen which then combines furiously with itself, or oxygen, or anything else in range, to form unwieldly molecules. A proton beam fired from the ground could be expected to be 100,000,000 times weaker near the top of the atmosphere, by which time it would also have been scattered over a wide area. The resulting beam would be too feeble to cause noticeable damage.

There *are* possible ways around these difficulties – such is Man's ingenuity when an interesting new weapon is mooted. To destroy a weapon with a ground-based beam, it has been suggested that first we drill a hole in the atmosphere to fire the beam through! In practice this means that the accelerator is rapidly pulsed to heat up a long column of air, which becomes a column of highly energised plasma which offers less resistance to the beam. (Compare the difference between firing a bullet through water and through a cloud of steam.) Within this column of air – perhaps a couple of centimetres across – heated to many thousands of degrees, the proton beam would be attenuated only very slightly. The fresh trouble is that *because* of the ionisation of this air-column, the beam could lash about to follow an irregular path: who has seen a straight-line lightning bolt? This presents one or two difficulties of aiming.

As usual, our atmosphere is the villain – or the peacekeeper, depending on one's viewpoint – and it seems again that a workable proton beam weapon must be sited out in space. Tentative plans for such a setup have been outlined, although more in a spirit of *reductio ad absurdum* argument against the idea than as serious considerations of a likely weapon. A 5GeV proton beam has been suggested, which would fire 10 bursts per second at ICBMs as they rose, each burst delivering an energy of some 10,000,000 joules. Such an assault could rapidly melt many metals (e.g., aluminium), and could certainly destroy missile electronics. the feasibility of such a beam weapon is best studied through comparison with conventional particle accelerators. The 400 GeV proton synchrotron at CERN (*Conseil Européen pour la Recherche Nucléaire* – now European Organisation for Nuclear Research, in Geneva) can even now deliver proton bursts with a total energy of a million joules or more, although not as yet with the required frequency – CERN's limit is presently one burst per 8 seconds as opposed to the desired 10 per second. CERN is also a little large to be put into orbit – the main synchrotron ring is a kilometre and a half in diameter – but with luck the machine could be condensed to a few metres across by using lower proton energies and more powerful (e.g., superconducting) deflector magnets to keep the beam circulating in the accelerator ring. To compensate for the lower energy we need higher beam intensity (less energetic protons, but more of them) than CERN, perhaps a hundred times higher, which cannot be directly provided by such accelerators, at least as we build them today. But even this can be contrived by using a storage ring – also in use at CERN – which the accelerator can pump full of fast protons for discharge in a single lethal burst. The size of the hypothetical satellite installation has now doubled, a storage ring being about the same size as its feeding accelerator. Additional delays are now caused to the superweapon by the fact that the storage ring takes time to charge up. Using CERN as the model once again, we can expect the ring to take half an hour to fill, after which the dreaded beam weapon will be ready to fire; and half an hour later, to fire again. And all along we assume that the needed megawatts of accelerator power can be supplied . . .

The beam weapon has not come to the end of its problems. Just as artificial magnetic fields bend the proton beam in a synchrotron, other fields can bend it outside – the Earth's field, for example, is likely to produce deviations of whole degrees when the range is in thousands of kilometres. Finally, this large and expensive installation would be a prime target in its own right – it would spend its time in self-defence until overwhelmed. But, like the laser weapon, the particle beam will not be abandoned until proven *definitely* unworkable. For example, some of the electromagnetic problems – beam spread through particle repulsion, deflection in the Earth's field – might just be overcome by using a *neutral*-particle beam. The US Sipapu project (the word is American Indian and means sacred fire) is working towards a beam of initially charged hydrogen molecules which will be neutralised *after* acceleration to high energy. The atmosphere may still be a barrier to such a beam (though there are reports that it's thought of as, ultimately, a ground-based as well as a space-based weapon); the possibilities in space are immense.

III : Exotica

Wierd and fantastic weaponry always makes for interesting reading; elaboration and exoticism for their own sakes are not, however, likely to win favour with military planners. No matter how elegant an application of physics or ingenious a piece of engineering the weapon may be, there's little point in using it on the battlefield unless it is more cost-effective (in terms of deaths, incapacitations or military value of property destroyed per unit capital expenditure) than the mechanisms which have become established over the years. A good example is (once again) that old notion of a hand-held death ray; long considered impossible, the device could now be built after a fashion. Its user would wear massive cylinders upon his back to supply the CO_2 or hydrogen and fluorine required, connected by heavy, flexible tubes to the 'hand weapon' itself. This main body might be around the size of a bag of golf-clubs, although heavier. Each burst of laser radiation therefrom would be lethal at ranges up to, say, a few hundred metres and capable of dazzling or blinding at greater distances. Although the CO_2 and HF lasers theoretically give continuous output, a cooling-off period between bursts will be needed, else the weapon becomes too hot to hold. There only remains the problem of the deadly exhaust from an HF laser (our hero would have to wear something not unlike a spacesuit), or the pre-heating requirement of a CO_2 laser of the gas-dynamic variety. There goes the supertechnological soldier, staggering cumbrously forward to wreak destruction on anyone he can entice within range ... meanwhile, the despicable enemy has opened fire with an old-fashioned but extremely cheap and efficient sub-machine gun.

It seems that weird weapons must fall under one of three headings. They may actually provide a new and cost-effective means of destroying or harassing the enemy. They may have peculiar advantages of range, convenience or speed which, despite cost considerations, makes them useful for special work: the laser missile-killing satellite could be one such, and assassination weapons are not concerned with cost-effectiveness. Finally, they may be low-intensity weapons which produce minimal casualties, of use when the wielder does *not* wish to kill – the classic situation being that of 'peaceful' riot control.

Most novel weapons available in the first category have already been considered. One which has not is the Fuel Air Explosive (FAE) bomb, whose continuing refinement seems likely to help extend the destructive power of conventional weapons to meet that of the smaller uclear bombs. FAE is not really new; there was some British research on its possibilities during World War II, although that war ended before the weapon was perfected. These first FAE devices were simply metal drums containing a mixture of petroleum and compressed methane gas. When the drum was dropped it would burst, releasing the gas and liquid, which expanded and evaporated respectively into a moderately large cloud. Then, before it could disperse, this gas-cloud would be ignited by a timed incendiary device, producing an explosion over a considerable area. The effect can be as if a very large bomb has been dropped – much larger than the container which is actually used.

The first combat use of FAE was in Vietnam in the mid-60s. By then the principle had been refined; the fuel/explosive was now ethylene oxide, which is highly volatile and burns spontaneously without any need for oxygen. (This eliminates part of the ignition timing problem; with the petroleum/methane bomb it was necessary to calculate the moment when the gases had mingled with air sufficiently to become highly explosive. Delay would lead to their dispersal in the air.) The standard FAE bomb was the BLU-73, using ethylene oxide, which could detonate mines and defoliate trees in a circle about thirty metres across – the blast would of course be deadly well outside this circle. A larger weapon, the CBU-55, combined three BLU-73s which spread out (like re-entry vehicles from a MIRV carrier) to bracket a target with FAE explosions. It appears that present-day FAE bombs deliver about five times the explosive force, weight for weight, as TNT – and this ratio is being increased. A future warhead carrying a couple of hundred pounds of FAE explosive may be equivalent to a one-ton TNT warhead, which is moving 'conventional' explosions towards the nuclear range. There is no reason why much larger FAE weapons could not be built. The diplomatic consequences could be unpleasant – if 'going nuclear' retains its present horror and a super-FAE is used, *will* the enemy believe that this is a mere conventional weapon?

Another important development is not a weapon but a delivery system which could vastly alter the present nuclear stalemate. This is the cruise missile, a small and relatively cheap device which can be launched from practically anywhere (aircraft, submarine, wheeled vehicle) and is equipped to scan the terrain and compute an extremely precise course to its target. Many forms of warhead are possible – gas, small nuclear weapons, FAE, conventional explosives or incendiaries. Further consideration of the cruise missile in use is deferred to the next chapter; for now, it should be noted that with the cheap, mass-production methods which could be used to manufacture cruise missiles with FAE warheads – without the immense cost, precision-engineering and dirtiness of 'nukes' – they could offer any nation, no matter how poor, the ability to destroy on a huge scale . . . Presently it appears that the most significant improvements in warfare are minor, peripheral matters or carefully calculated steps backward: we may have the ultimate weapons in the form of nuclear-tipped ICBMs, but there are enormous difficulties in getting them to their targets and still vaster political reasons for not using them at all. The concept of 'small is beautiful' may, ironically, apply. Highly destructive but non-nuclear systems like the FAE cruise-missile offer the possibility of doing damage of near-nuclear proportions while remaining within the letter of the law: 'nuclear use is unthinkable'.

The use of technology in espionage and assination mostly boils down to simple and unedifying matters of electronic miniaturisation – especially of bugging devices – cryptanalysis and coercion ('The subject still being reticent, a measure of electronic coercion was applied to his testicles'), with only occasional forays into the more romantic world of silenced weapons and ingenious booby-traps. Science fiction offers interesting notions for hand-to-hand combat, like built-in 'body armour' under the skin and a multitude of small combat aids like John Brunner's *Karatand*, a glove of soft plastic which stiffens on impact (like 'silly putty') to make the hand a deadly weapon. *C'est magnifique mais ce n'est pas la guerre.*

The same applies, really, to the use of technology for riot control and similar situations. Here we deal with a supposedly precise use of force to subdue without, in theory, causing lasting harm. Unfortunately there are very few means of control which cannot inflict severe injury or cause death. The 'harmless' gases such as CS, intended to incapacitate rioters or besieged criminals without injury, have a way of building up in enclosed spaces to become extremely toxic: of course, any gas is toxic in sufficient concentration, even oxygen. Worse, in every crowd there will be heart cases, asthmatics and people who are just very susceptible to a given gas. This has led to some consideration of other possibilities, many of them at a rudimentary technological level such as Cold Brine Projectors (but the impact of water-jets at close range can be quite injurious) and rubber bullets, which can also cause serious injury. Among the exotic suggestions is the 'taser', perhaps the nearest approach so far to science fiction's standard stun-gun. It fires a small barbed projectile which is supposed to catch in the victim's clothing. A thin wire leads back to the main body of the weapon, and pulses of electric current at moderately high voltage go out along the wire (the technology thus combines the spring-gun and the electric-fence circuitry used to discourage escapist cows). This subdues the victim; once in a while, of course, he or she will be subdued to the extent of a heart-attack.

More ambitious means of discouraging mobs were suggested. Subsonic vibrations, too low for the ear to detect, can induce strange sensations in people; at frequences from 5 to 13 cycles per second (Hz) resonances are set up within the human body. Fear and unease are experienced by victims; also headaches and abdominal pain. (A sense of panic can produce sinking feelings in the gut; here the feelings are generated directly to affect the mind by association.) High levels of subsound are required to produce these effects; again the problem is that actual damage (e.g., haemorrhage) can be caused to people too close to the generator, not to mention that suffered by those trampled beneath a panicked crowd. The 'photic driver' attempts to avoid damage by relying not on intensity but quality of effect. Here a bank of flickering lights – not consciously perceived, being outside the optical range – is used to cause odd effects of unease – compare with the hypnotic flicker of strobe lights at certain frequencies like 5 Hz. Infrared penetrates the eyelids, so that shutting the eyes is useless. The result could be confusion, mild trance, fainting, tremors – and, in those prone to them, epileptic fits. This is not at all acceptable.

We have considered the present-day weapons applications of a large number of physical principles – kinetic energy and inertia, chemical energy, sound and light, nuclear processes and the radiations they produce. To conclude this chapter there follows a list of less immediately likely possibilities.

Atmospheric scattering is one of the great problems of radiation weapons: it can be shown that scattering effects are proportional to the fourth power of the radiation frequency – i.e., inversely proportional to the fourth power of the wave-length. This is why the sky appears blue; blue (higher frequency) sunlight is scattered about the sky by air molecules to a much greater extent than the red part of the light, leaving the direct light of the Sun a little deficient in blue so that it appears yellowish. For this reason infrared (IR) lasers should penetrate the air best, and would always do so but for freak absorptions by CO_2 and water vapour at some frequencies. Ultraviolet (UV) light, theoretically more damaging, is scattered considerably more and, with contemporary laser technology, is much more difficult to produce at high intensity. So, although UV is more damaging than visible light when we compare photon for photon, there are fewer photons to start with and a smaller proportion reach the target than for IR. (The atmosphere successfully screens out virtually all of the higher-frequency rays of the Sun.) X-rays are still more energetic but can only be produced, now, by nuclear weapons or atomic processes involving beams of high-energy electrons impacting metal targets; X-ray laser is easy to consider, but it's highly uncertain that one can be built – how, among other problems, do we make mirrors for rays which pass happily through steel?

Another range of radiation not so far discussed is the microwave band, of lower frequency than IR but higher than radio waves. Microwaves can have a direct effect on matter when sufficiently intense, as seen in the microwave oven, where the strong microwave absorption in water is used to heat water-containing foodstuffs. (There is still stronger absorption in alcohol; Professor N. Kurti of Oxford invented the 'inverted Baked Alaska' whose outer layers of ice-cream conceal a core of marmalade laced with brandy, selectively microwave-heated to the amazement of gourmets.) Naturally such radiation can be injurious to human tissue, as persons sterilised by defective microwave ovens have discovered, but the old bugbear of atmospheric absorption works again – over any significant distance the beam energy is expended on heating water-vapour in the air. Besides, at these long wavelengths – centimetres – diffraction effects mean that the beam will inevitably spread, even in space, far more rapidly than visible light. Radar installations may pump megawatts of microwave radiation into the sky – enough to cook people at close range – only to receive mere microwatts of echo from aircraft or missiles for which they scan. Meanwhile, there is presently some concern about the damaging effects of low-level microwaves over a period of time. If only one could persuade the hostile army to stand still for twenty years while one showered them with debilitating microwaves (as the USSR are reputed to have done to the US embassy in Moscow) and offered them debilitating cigarettes!

Perhaps the final present possibility for non-material weapons is the magnetic field. An oscillating field of sufficient intensity can induce electric currents in metals, and heat them to a level dependent on the field strength, the oscillation frequency and the properties of the metal. This is the principle of the induction furnace, where metal contained in a magnetic coil will melt without an apparent heat-source. There is also the fictional 'Dentichar handgun, whose supermagnetic induction pulse caused the victim's fillings to glow white-hot' (a sobering thought). However, magnetic field intensity falls off very rapidly as the distance from the 'source' increases – the field is not a thing in its own right, like the photon, but a property of moving charges (as electrostatic fields are associated with any charges, moving or stationary, and gravitational fields with matter). It seems unlikely that meltig of metal could be achieved at more than a few metres, or interference with electronics at more than a few tens of metres. (This does still leave open the possibility of an electromagnetic defence – an induction field which puffs bullets into vapour as they approach.) I might repeat Haldane's words on heat-rays and suggest that any coil powerful enough to send out such a field at reasonable range 'would not merely melt, but explode into fiery gas in a tiny fraction of a second' owing to the tremendous currents – tremendous movements of charge – required to produce the field. But there are such things as superconductors, and like Haldane I could easily be wrong.

CHAPTER FOUR

WAR IN NEAR SPACE

I: The Orbital Watch

The space of seven continued nights he rode
With darkness, thrice the equinoctial line
He circled, four times cross'd the car of night
From pole to pole, traversing each colure . . .
MILTON, *Paradise Lost*, IX

For thousands of kilometres out from the fringes of our atmosphere, near space is littered with free-falling products of human technology. They range in size from nuts and bolts to the complete, burnt-out shells of rocket stages. From time to time such fragments slip back into the atmosphere; falling faster and faster, they are heated by friction and expire in hot flashes of vaporised metal.

The balance of forces which holds this litter up is identical to that which keeps the Moon from falling to the Earth, or the Earth into the Sun. Any two masses tend to fly together, as Newton recorded in his Law of Universal Gravitation; at the same time, the general sluggishness of matter makes it prefer to continue in a straight line – in the direction along which it was first travelling. The Moon travels sideways and would 'like' to move off at a tangent to its orbit round Earth; even as it does so, gravity causes it to fall a little *towards* the Earth. The combined effect of the downward and sideways motions produces a curved, balanced orbit, never falling to Earth and never quite escaping.

In circles or ellipses, each body of the Solar System

moves around another, and all of them around the Sun, a stately dance which has continued for many millions of years. It would be depressing to think that the junk we have strewn beyond out atmosphere is liable to endure as a menace to space-traffic for so long – longer yet than the half-life of the dread plutonium wastes! Fortunately the junk has not been placed with an eye to permanence. Most discarded bits never settle into orbit at all, but flash quickly down to ruin. Others, travelling in huge, eccentric ellipses which pass through the wispy outer fringes of the atmosphere, lose a little energy each time around; their orbits decay to the same ultimate fate. (The Solar System is stable because, or course, objects in grossly unstable orbits were weeded out long ago; smaller bits survive to provide an effectively unending stream of meteors.)

Surveillance and communications satellites are more carefully positioned, and can remain aloft for many years; a manned space-station, with the ability to make small corrections to its orbit when required, can maintain that orbit indefinitely. For scientific if not military reasons, a space-station has been wanted for some time; the long delays were the result of payload problems – the basic difficulty of pushing large masses of construction material for hundreds of kilometres, vertically. With the new space-shuttles, these huge cargoes become feasible. Abandoned fragments of orbital debris can be repossessed and used in the building of space-stations larger and more permanent than the fallen Skylab – which would not have fallen had it been manned and maintained.

The establishment of a permanent manned orbital station may, in future histories of space travel's origins, be noted as an achievement more truly significant than merely setting foot upon the Moon. All previous leapers into space have sooner or later fallen back; with a secure foothold beyond the atmosphere, we can expect a growing population which actually *lives* off Earth. The effect of this presence upon warfare is likely to be gradual and insidious . . .

Obvious advantages of carrying out research in orbit are the lack of gravity (to take a trivial example, one can in theory cast perfectly round ball-bearings) and the endless supply of good, hard vacuum. Operations such as electron-beam welding cannot be carried out in air, which scatters the beam before it can heat the weld; in orbit, the whole of space becomes a vacuum-chamber for such work. Another drawback of air is that it's difficult to see through; astronomers have long cursed the fluctuations of air-density which make the stars twinkle so prettily and so inconveniently. Orbital telescopes – as well as being free of gravitational stresses such as warp the mirrors of large earthbound observatories – will see the stars shining with a steady, unwavering light, in a sky which is never cloudy.

Telescopes can look inward as well as out, back to the Earth as well as to the heavens. 'The spirit of Man that goeth upward, and the spirit of the beast that goeth downward to the Earth.' That is a little unjust: exceedingly valuable information on crops and climate is gathered by camera-bearing satellites, which also have a more military application in tracing troop-movements and new constructions in hostile countries. Considering the size limitations of cameras aloft (picture quality depends largely on lens size) and the grainy TV images beamed down from these satellites through all manner of atmospheric interference, the amount of information which can be extracted is astonishing. US experts routinely use such surveillance to discover and guess at the purpose of new Soviet installations, even to individual buildings. No doubt the US – and the rest of the world – suffers a similar lack of privacy.

It is not hard to imagine the effects of replacing a 5 cm

camera lens with a 50 cm reflecting telescope, and the inefficiencies of video tubes and TV transmission with direct interpretation by the human eye (or perhaps advanced computer scanners). The only remaining obstacle to unrestricted spying are the miles of misty, wavering atmosphere between telescope and target. And, perhaps, the cunning of those victims of surveillance who camouflage their doings or contrive to go unobtrusively underground. The morality of this endless watch is a little uncertain. We can offer with equal conviction the argument that any invasion of privacy is evil (not a universally popular doctrine among today's governments) and the argument that, since international inspection of weapons stockpiles and levels of mobilisation is never likely to be agreed, watching from orbit is the next best thing.

The immediate effect of establishing such a permanent, unremitting watch is to make World War III just a little more unlikely. A possible attacker will be less eager to press his red buttons, in the knowledge that tireless computer eyes above would instantly note the launching of his ICBMs alerting the country under attack several minutes before the Distant Early Warning radar could emit the slightest squawk. In other words, although the outcome of nuclear war might be equally frightful, the supposed advantage of surprise is still further reduced. Launching the war from under cloud cover would not help the hypothetical attacker, since infrared scanners are perfectly able to spot the heat of missile-exhausts through the thickest cloud: besides, an ICBM must soon emerge from the clouds as it heads into space. Nor will a preliminary missile attack on the watching space-stations be useful, since the very attempt will warn its owners, whether or not the station were destroyed – and besides, minutes must again elapse between the launching and the strike.

The picture of a single space-station watching all the

Earth is of course simple-minded. In practice there would be one or more stations servicing a series of small satellites laden with the bulky, high-quality optical equipment which can only be assembled in orbit. Radio or microwave relay satellites would also be present, in case of breakdown of the existing communications satellites now internationally known. And since a single country will never be allowed to retain such an advantage, there will soon be two or more such orbital warning systems.

Different satellite orbits are suited to different purposes; the orbit into which an unpowered satellite falls depends upon its speed and direction. A perfectly circular path is rare – even the planets move in ellipses, swinging slowly nearer to or further from the Sun than the imaginary circles which for simplicity we call their orbits. Such ellipses are only slightly distorted circles; vaster, flatter, more eccentric paths are followed by comets, which may at the extremes of their motion skim close by the Sun and wander beyond the confines of the Solar System. (With sufficiently increased speed in the orbiting body, the ellipse opens into a hyperbola which curves out towards infinity, never returning.) In general, circular or almost-circular orbits are preferred for man-made satellites. Communications satellites normally follow the famous synchronous orbit, about 32,000 kilometres up; at this height the sideways speed or orbital velocity required to balance gravity is such that it takes the satellite just 24 hours to go around the Earth. Since Earth rotates at this same rate, it follows that a synchronous-orbit 'comsat' moving above the Equator will remain always over the same spot. The aiming of radio beams for satellite relay is thus always the same . . . Surveillance devices, meanwhile, tend to follow closer orbits with higher velocity, scanning rapidly across the Earth. Under the aegis of manned space-stations, the diversely orbiting satellites form a network of eyes and ears from which no major change or motion below may be hidden.

This covers the passive side of orbital war. A vantage point is established, a high place from which to study the kingdoms of the Earth. Historically, however, the exhilaration of looking down upon the doings of one's enemy is rapidly supplemented by the urge to drop something more or less unpleasant on his head. The early days of aerial reconnaissance in World War I showed the exhilaration, with English and German pilots waving to one another as they passed above the lines. It was not long before revolver-shots were exchanged between those planes, and crude 'jam-tin' bombs flung haphazardly down among the trenches; the gigantic machinery of war in the air had begun to move.

Like those frail aircraft, the space-stations with their satellite networks are unlikely, in the early days, to be more than a minor harassment to the serious business of warfare down below. And for the same reason: the first little planes were incapable of carrying weapons of significant size and power; and, although a few nuclear devices might be ferried into orbit, the innumerable tons of metal involved in modern arsenals will be too much for the available transport. Neither is the strategic advantage great — although they might be delivered a little earlier than long-range ICBMs hurtling across the pole, the necessary fewness of these bombs from orbit will make them mere gadflies. Minor nuisances, moreover, upon which the full wrath of enemy defences would be turned; when the defensive system is prepared for waves of hundreds or thousands of nuclear missiles (a first strike on the USSR, for example, could today consist of some 3000 US missiles and decoys) it's unlikely that even one of so few could make its strike.

Yet close-orbital space, where the final thin reaches of

the air have given place to vacuum, *is* a uniquely strategic zone. The powerful flight of an ICBM passes out into space at the peak of its trajectory, and at this time it is most vulnerable to attack. Ground-based interceptors are capable in theory of 'taking out' ICBMs outside the atmosphere, even with a near miss; but such anti-missile missiles are required to travel a considerable distance to their objective. And, if not stopped before re-entry, the ICBM-MIRV (Multiple Independently-Retargetable Vehicles) carriers are liable to release, as their name implies, several spearate missiles which will scatter to seek different targets below. The atmospheric interceptors ('terminal defence system') truly represent the last ditch, and it is imperative to minimise the load upon these: 'a stitch in time . . .' Therefore a logical question presents itself: can orbital installations attack ICBMs during their transit through space?

Interception-missiles based in orbit fall prey to the argument used against the dropping of bombs from orbit – one cannot place enough of them to be worthwhile. In the long run, perhaps, a system of orbiting nuclear mines might be established to cover ICBM launch windows. Such mines could disable or decimate the first wave of attacking missiles. The major effect of this capability is likely to be a surreptitious increase in nuclear armament, to the point where even the first wave of ICBMs will more than adequately saturate this defence. For an affluent country, proliferation of offensive weapons along these lines is the standard strategic answer to any interception system of less than 100% effectiveness.

But near space provides the first practicable battle-ground for the science-fictional energy weapons considered in the last chapter. There is thee huge particle accelerator, which would force large numbers of protons to enormous velocities; stationed in synchronous orbit, the device is theoretically capable of emitting proton beams of an intensity to melt metal or at least wreck the electronics of missiles at great distances. Admittedly it would be difficult to aim such a beam, or to compensate for its bending in the Earth's magnetic field, or to provide the multi-megawatt power supply required by the accelerator. These problems are merely technical: the apparently insuperable ones are the low firing rate (several minutes between firings is the best that can be hoped for, as compared with a military requirement of at least ten shots per second) and the ease with which this whole monstrous installation could be blown out of the sky.

The need is for small, fast weapons – fast to aim and fast to fire. Ideally these should be scattered across near space in shoals of little satellites, each independently powered by its conversion of sunlight to electricity, all linked by tight radio beams (*via* relay satellites where necessary) to the computer co-ordinating these defences. If all these qualities could be combined with a degree of deadliness sufficient to disable an ICBM with a single shot, a worthwhile orbital defence would be available.

These requirements match closely the lasers we may expect in the near future. The key element is the CO_2 or hydrogen-fluoride laser amplifier, which can produce for brief periods a tremendous output of coherent light or infrared radiation. A small advance on existing technology will provide a beam capable of punching holes through the re-entry capsule of an ICBM. Satellite-mounted and fired by a radio-directed micro-computer, a pulsed laser of this type would suffer only from the drawback of low firing-rate – solar panels may provide free power, but not enough to match the tempo of missile interception. But with this small system, which unlike the giant proton accelerator could be suited to relatively cheap mass-production, the time between pulses is irrelevant provided that enough such lasers are in operation. The effective firing rate may be made as rapid as required by adding more laser satellites and directing all of them to fire in sequence.

At this point it's possible to imagine an action fought at such a level of technology. The eyes above note happenings on the ground: they see the points of fire break out across a continent as the launches begin. Then very slowly the vapour-trails crawl upward, towards the North Pole in their great arch whose top will protrude into space. The jammed radar systems crackle and flash with interference; but compressed, digitised information stutters across the tight communication beams (perhaps small lasers themselves) from satellite to satellite, passing data to Orbital Command's space-station and returning coded orders to the weapons carriers, orders based upon computer extrapolations of the accurate, optically tracked missile courses . . . The fighting is not dramatic. No beams of incandescence slash through space, there being nothing to diffuse the laser light and betray its presence – but as each laser fires, a star of diffracted light shows brief and intolerable at the aperture. A steadier glow comes from the tails of the missiles; little clouds of bright-lurid smoke puff momentarily from their long bodies, where laser strikes have vaporised the surface material. A silent flash, and one ICBM is expanding gas and fragments: a direct hit on the explosive trigger of its warhead. Another, with the bulkier, deadlier MIRV appearance, plunges to re-entry . . . There is a faint sigh of relief in Orbital Command as it continues to plunge, dead, safe, not splitting into vicious independent missiles. It vanishes into the huge blue-and-white disc of Earth. A hit on the electronics package, perhaps: how is one to know? There are more noiseless explosions, fast and unreal . . . But another attacker slips through, glowing red from friction as it falls and falls, until at length there is a flash on the ground more brilliant than any yet seen. And below, a tall cloud of sufficiently familiar shape. The Orbital Command station makes ready for the second wave.

This battle is unlikely to be fought. As it stands, it relies on the assumption that one country or alliance reigns more or less unchallenged in space, and has been able to set up its elaborate system of laser-armed satellites without opposition. It is far more probable that a sort of orbital arms race will ensue, and that various moves to neutralise satellite weaponry would form the first stage of an attack. The space-stations seem particularly vulnerable and, despite their own formidable defences (lasers and perhaps some small missiles), are not strong positions; a saturation attack upon them would have a good chance of success. A laser can deactivate a missile aimed directly at the station – but a pressurised construction in space is vulnerable even to the inert lump of material which remains hurtling towards it. Or some simpler, more treacherous means of destroying them may be possible. The amount of intrigue and chicanery possible in space, where there are no borders or customs checks, is staggering. And so a skirmish as simple as that described is an exceedingly remote possibility.

However cunning the countermeasures, the mere presence – or the mere possibility – of a laser defence ring is bound to weaken the credibility of the ICBM as an effective weapon. An orbital arms race may prove one of those curious dead ends of warfare – vast efforts rendered useless by a blind spot in the basic reasoning, such as the impregnable Maginot Line. It may be that one Great Power will happily allow the others to defend the immense stable door of near space, and meanwhile discard the ICBM entirely.

An ICBM is ludicrously expensive. Enormous energy is used in carrying the payload clean out of the atmosphere, in order to reach the target in the minimum possible time. Even greater is the cost of the colossal underground silos which conceal these monsters until their hypothetical hour of use. Neither does one get particularly good value for money: the unwieldiness of the vehicle makes it moderately easy to intercept and capable of only limited evasive action (the MIRV is one attempt to counter this difficulty). Strategists have for some time been dissatisfied with these giant phallic symbols, and would be enthusiastic for their gradual complete abandonment, provided there were a cheap and convenient substitute.

The proposed substitute is the cruise missile. It's another mass-production weapon, reminiscent of the old German V-1 with a few refinements. The most important feature is a microcomputer 'brain' made possible by recent electronic technology – a black box which can be programmed with details of landscape and with this information fly the missile in hedge-hopping fashion, below the heights at which radar is effective, to strike a target thousands of miles distant – accurately to within some tens of metres. Evasion tactics of any reasonable degree of complexity can be included in the programme . . .

Thanks to the accuracy of cruise missiles, they can carry small 'cost-effective' nuclear warheads, or FAE, or even conventional explosives where real selectivity is required. They are cheap to produce and can be amassed in such numbers as to overwhelm any existing defence system (even the micro-computer need not be more expensive to mass-produce than the better electronic calculators). They are small: up to 20 may be carried by a modern bomber, and even more by a submarine. All in all, in a world of shrinking defence allocations, cruise missiles would appear to be the strategist's dream. Those persons likely to be on the receiving end may welcome them with less enthusiasm.

It must be remembered, though, that this is a short-term

argument. The cruise missile may emerge to reign supreme for years or decades; but inevitably, something else will turn up. For example, low-flying cruise missiles would be highly vulnerable to ground-based laser cannon or to tiny 'intelligent' interceptors which have wide orders of magnitude smaller and cheaper than those needed to tackle ICBMs. Until a decisive war is actually fought, the slow battle for superiority in offence and defence is unending.

Meanwhile, the ICBM retains the advantage of being rapid, powerful, tested and feared. Whatever the merits of cruise-missiles – however ingenious the orbital interception – however monstrous the continuing maintenance costs – ICBMs will remain with us for a long while, bulwarked by the sheer inertia of policy and the sheer magnitude of existing investment. The need for orbital defences may eventually fade with the ICBM, but the advantages of observation – of, for example, pin-pointing from above the vapour-trail of cruise missiles – will remain until the as yet incredible ground-based lasers form a defense against *all* missile attack. Meanwhile in the age of the cruise missile, the men of the Orbital Command station might find themselves cast as spectators, watching the vapour-trails writhe like sinuous worms across land and sea, able to do no more than pass data to ground-based defences until, perhaps, a swarm of ace-in-the-hole ICBMs comes thundering up to put an end to this invasion of privacy.

II: The Orbital Chessboard

Wickedness is always easier than virtue, for it takes the short cut to everything.

DR JOHNSON

This chapter has so far considered situations of watchful peace and total war, with a lightning transit from the first to the second. In practice nuclear war may be more likely to develop slowly from smaller frictions below – from the escalation of minor conflicts to which in their early stages are classified merely as 'military aid', 'police actions' or 'limited conventional war'. The Great Powers are sufficiently aware of this, and under normal circumstances will do all they can to avoid nuclear intervention; the cost of putting such an end to a minor war would almost certainly be involvement in a major and perhaps a 'final' one. For similar reasons, considerable hanky-panky will have to take place in orbit before ground-based ICBMs are brought into play.

Are there strong enough motives for some country to indulge in dubious tactics – for example, sabotage? The diplomacy of space is young and uncertain, the associated emotions not yet smothered in precedent. The risk would be very high, however much a fear of nuclear war might buffer the reactions; on the other hand, the rewards could also be worthwhile. For example: The foremost specimens of miniaturised electronics, outside a country's research laboratories, may be found in the hardware of its satellites. If the early speculations of this chapter are justified, many satellites will contain not only tempting examples of state-of-the-art microelectronics, but also a particularly advanced form of laser weapon. These units are behind no national borders ('Space is international'), surrounded by no security fences: they hang in orbit like ripe plums. Why trouble with the tortuous wiles of espionage, a rival power might reason, when one has only to reach out?

Naturally this is over-simplified – hardware in orbit is closely watched, tracked from the ground and (in the proposed scenario) linked into an orbital radar and communications network which might overlook the falling of an occasional sparrow, but scarcely anything larger. The possibility of accident, however, cannot be denied. The odds against a satellite's being struck by a meteor are very large (smaller than those against meteor strikes on craft in free space, since Earth's gravity pulls in a good deal of assorted debris), but they cannot be discounted by its owners. They, the owners, may be quite aware that such a convenient 'accident' might easily be caused by – say – a shell or the equivalent from some other satellite whose orbit passed close for a moment to that of the vanished unit; but, in either case, the laser satellite has been disabled and diverted from its known orbit. Likewise, it can only be assumed that the lost unit fell to a fiery end in Earth's sky; the manoeuvres far below of a rival's space-shuttle may have been mere coincidence. The detection through ground radar of a falling, flaming object would be an established fact; it would surely seem over-suspicious to hint that a swift exchange had been made, that the missing satellite was in transit to enemy laboratories even as a hundred kilograms of substituted scrap-iron fell glowing through the upper air.

As well as the meteor-accident theory, there would also remain the possibility of a hit by one of those pieces of orbiting junk previously mentioned – although the large and useful items might be seized as building material for space-stations, smaller fragments in uncharted orbits would linger; tools and scrap mislaid in the assembly of the stations themselves, excreta dumped by earlier missions (the stations themselves will no doubt recycle their wastes), and perhaps some relics of orbital explosions and other accidents, the macabre fragments quick-frozen and preserved . . . The intricate criss-cross of intersecting and interweaving orbits will always contain a few surprises.

So a well planned act of sabotage or theft might be difficult indeed to prove. Little private reservations would still be made by the victim, and perhaps a decision would be taken to retaliate in kind. A gradually escalating Cold War in orbit is conceivable, with the mounting of conventional weapons in space-stations under one pretext or another, with defences and booby-traps built into important satellites. The security of a satellite could for example be protected by an explosive sharge, set to detonate a certain period after the satellite is distributed (unless it is disarmed by a hidden procedure). Should such a booby-trap explode within the capturing vehicle, it would be the kidnappers' turn to grit their teeth and remain silent . . . and to make some further little private plans. The most unfortunate irony of all would be the development of this growing snowball of tension, doubt and minor crisis from an accident which was, after all, pure accident.

The overt actions of such orbital rivalry must remain quiet and small. At these high levels – both physical and political – it's needful to move most cautiously. This applies especially in the case where two powers, no more, have occupied space between them; should others join them there, confusion and ambiguity will increase. Example: Swinging back in from an elliptical orbit beyond the scanning-range of radar, an unidentified satellite approaches some expensive installation and explodes destructively. Who is responsible? Who knows? In the growing climate of suspicion (metaphorical climates are the only ones to be found in vacuum), space-station defences are augmented with mirror-shields to deflect lasers; some modified form of ground-to-air or air-to-air missile is devised to break through such mirrors; interceptor missiles to defend against these . . . Explosive 'killer satellites', intended specifically for use against other satellites in orbit, are already being tested. But a full-scale conventional war in orbit could be as politically explosive as nuclear on the ground below. Fascinating though the tactics of actual combat might become, with armed descendants of the space-shuttle manoeuvring subtly from one orbital level to another, there remains a tacit restriction to 'police actions' and suchlike, against saboteurs disowned by their own countries.

However 'unthinkable' it may be convenient to call a further world war, astute antagonists will be careful to consider every possibility. The simplest view of Total War involves the nightmarish theory of 'pre-emptive strike', whereby one attempts to blast one's opponent before he makes his attack – or perhaps before he has even considered making an attack. Part of the advantage in this is nullified, as already discussed, by the network of orbital watchers which reduces dramatically the interval between initial firing and the alerting of the victim. Therefore the Orbital Command space-stations must be removed from the scene as the first action of such a strike, before damning data can be relayed to the ground defences.

A simple approach would be through a satellite whose ostensible purpose was secondary to the nuclear weapon concealed deep in its vitals. No traffic rules have been laid down for space; the owners of the target installation could do no more than insist that the orbit of this dubious satellite crosses the station's at a respectful distance. With a multi-megaton explosion, complete and virtually instantaneous destruction could be achieved across a separation of kilometres when the hour came around. That hour would be calculated to occur when the bulk of Earth lay between the station and its mother-country, preventing the tell-tale star from flaming in those skies. Of course, the Orbital Command station might orbit syschronously above some point in its own country. There might exist several such stations, with automatic backups concealed in unlikely orbits. And the neutron radiation of that orbiting plutonium warhead could quite possibly be detected – which would be embarrasing. The strategy of this third world war will not be simple.

And what of the tactics of combat between space-stations? In brief: It doesn't seem likely that space-stations will trouble to indulge in combat. The 'Orbital Command' station suggested here is more analogous to a radar system than to a warship: a key element of defence which may become a target, but is not seriously intended to take the offensive. It has the advantage of relative inaccessibility – a pre-emptive strike against it would be difficult indeed to bring off without losing the advantage of surprise so essential to such a move. Unless the attack is sdden, anonymous and completely successful, it is not worthwhile. A ground-based attack can be neither sudden nor anonymous (the origins of launches would be routinely noted, and the arrival predicted sufficient minutes in advance . . .); attack from orbit is uncertain of success for the reasons suggested above. The observation network, it seems, will be safe if sufficiently well designed – e.g., able to function without one or more of its command centres – and so, with the advantage of surprise devalued, a final war remains a little less likely than before.

Despite the above, it's obvious that the space-station programme will not be an entirely warlike concern. War in the near future remains essentially an affair of the ground – or at any rate the atmosphere – space is a convenient grandstand from which to observe the antics below.

Propelling vast masses of weaponry into space so that they may fall again to Earth *is* a waste or energy; this forms the major argument against ICBMs and, for that matter, the hordes of satellite-borne doomsday weapons which were feared only a few years ago. Strategists and military planners, forced by circumstances into a grisly form of cost-accountancy, demand value for the public's money in terms of megadeaths per currency unit; the heavy engines of brute force remain economically below while space concerns itself with reconnaissance, with research, and with preparation.

A foothold has been established beyond the atmosphere. There is the opportunity for experiments in depth and at length upon the performance of men and machinery in this hostile world of airlessness and weightlessness. Provided only that the coming about of the unthinkable does not leave our spacemen staring glumly down at a ruined Earth, all will be ready for a further reaching-out, with its own fresh problems of technology and of strategy: the colonisation of space.

CHAPTER FIVE

COERCING NATURE

I: Fire and Water

And if the sky and sea be foes,
We will tame the sea and sky.
G. K. CHESTERTON, *The Ballad of the White Horse*

The cataclysmic effects of nuclear weapons beg for comparison with the natural disasters of historical times – events which produce the most horrifying destruction without resorting to a sudden release of those 'ultimate' forces locked within the nucleus. One of history's most spectacular explosions (although since outstripped by man-made weapons) was not the result of any dealing on the nuclear level but almost literally a greatly magnified boiler explosion . . . this was the celebrated eruption of Krakatoa (between Java and Sumatra) in 1883.

Krakatoa had always been a volcanic island with a history of eruptions; from 1877, a regular rumbling of earthquakes could be felt all about it. May 1883 saw renewed eruptions from the volcanic cone itself, with pumice, dust and smoke being flung into the air while the ground became noticeably warm. This went on for weeks, until in late August the island literally exploded. The four most violent detonations all took place within a few hours; the total effect seems to have been in the megaton range. In surged the sea, only to boil off in an inferno of lava and superheated steam. Only a small portion of one edge of the original volcanic crater remained; subterranean steam explosions had blown masses of rock and pumice into the air, until the island, which had risen 425 metres above sea level, was replaced for the most part by a pit 300 metres below. Close on six cubic *kilometres* of earth and rock were blasted free of the island; having been hurled 27 kilometres into the air, the great masses of rubble smashed old islands nearby and piled up to form new ones; meanwhile, a 15-metre tidal wave wiped out towns, villages and tens of thousands of people. The ash and smoke darkened the sky 150 kilometres away (lamps had to be lit at noon), and 300 kilometres away the eruption's shockwave rocked houses; the sound of the four great explosions could be heard at 5000 kilometres. The most lingering remnants, clouds of fine dust in the stratosphere, coloured the world's sunsets with lurid beauty for nearly a year.

And all this titanic display was caused by a boiler explosion. Water from the sea, it seems, had gradually seeped down into the molten magma within the Earth's crust, there to be vaporised and superheated, developing huge pressure. Something eventually had to give way and (as had happened at least twice before) it was Krakatoa which provided what might with a certain black irony be called a safety-valve. It is within the power of human technology to set off comparable or larger explosions – to blast a 300-metre-deep crater as was left in place of Krakatoa should take a medium-sized fusion bomb with a yield of 30–40 megatons; that is, 1500 to 2000 times the nominal yield of the Hiroshima bomb. But, as has been noted more than once, there is a strong reluctance to fling around fusion bombs or even the relatively puny tactical devices, for fear of escalation. It is conceivable that a sufficiently unscrupulous power might look long and hard at volcanic areas in unfriendly countries. Might it not be possible to give the natural order of things a nudge – to stimulate an eruption where none is due? In principle: yes.

The basis of advanced weapon systems is the import-
ation of new and potent energy-sources into a conflict,
extending the destructive power of their human controllers.
Chemical energy is locked in all explosives, awaiting release
through detonation so that a finger on the trigger can
unleash vastly more force than humanly exerted; with
nuclear weapons the 'trigger' is harder to pull (some
kilograms of Pu-239 must be forced into a tiny sphere) and
the work is done at two removes by explosives. The energy
of a sleeping volcano is likewise locked away: in a way it is
nuclear energy, since the Earth's inner heat is maintained
by the continuing radioactive decay of millions on millions
of tons of unstable elements in the mantle and core.
According to the theory of plate tectonics, the crust of the
Earth is composed of many separate 'plates' tens of
kilometres thick, which move over the layers below at the
rate of centimetres per year; fresh material is forced up at
the mid-ocean ridges, and the edges of the plates sink again
where they collide and overlap; e.g., around the Pacific. In
zones of rising or sinking, or where the plates grind slowly
against one another, there are earthquakes and fault-
systems which allow molten rock to be forced up from the
deeps. When a passage to the surface is found, there is a
great release of gases and smoke; lava is forced to the
surface and successive emissions may build up the
characteristic volcanic cone, while the subterranean
turmoil shakes the ground about. It seems that truly
colossal volcanic explosions (like that of Krakatoa or,
perhaps five times as powerful, the eruption of Thēra near
Crete which erased the Minoan culture and probably gave
rise to the legends of Atlantis) are produced when water
and molten lava meet to result in vast overpressures of
superheated steam. In some cases seepage of water through
the rocks may generate this deadly steam; in others, as at

Krakatoa, a preliminary 'conventional' eruption opens the way to the sea and the holocaust.

Is this, then, the recipe for a Krakatoa-scale blast? One drills unobtrusively to the appropriate depth, installs extremely heavy-duty pumps and forces water down towards the seething magma. The water vaporises to steam and develops tremendous pressure: presently it finds its own outlet. This is why the pump must be heavy-duty, or course; all this effort is not being expended in order to blow off the pump-head and create a scalding geyser. A little rough calculation gives the approximate hydraulics of such a scheme. If we wish the pressure developed to lift one cubic kilometre of rock weighing some 2,200,000,000 tons, the pressure over an area of one square kilometre needs to be some 4,400,000 atmospheres. The force developed is proportional to the area over which the pressure acts; if the pumping were done through a pipeline with an area of ten square centimetres, the force up the pipeline would be a relatively puny few hundred tons weight. The engineering problems would be great, even without considering the effect of the molten magma upon the drilling system, etc.; but engineering problems have a way of being overcome by ingenuity of brute force when the need is great – or thought to be great.

The real objection to volcano-triggering arises from the lack of suitable sites . . . places where there is both some volcanic action and some installation of strategic importance. Generally the volcanic potential drives people away (lest they find themselves trapped by inconvenient circumstances such as afflicted the townsfolk of Pompeii) and is a certain deterrent to the establishment of military sites. Active volcanic areas are concentrated in the 'Ring of Fire' around the Pacific plus other scattered sites such as Iceland and parts of the Mediterranean (Vesuvius, Etna, Stromboli, Vulcano). The US and USSR are virtually devoid of volcanic sites, as is most of Europe. Japan, with its 54 active or recent volcanoes, might be susceptible to tampering – and a little work on Popocatépetl could wreak havoc in Mexico Cito – but generally the 'weapon' has no military value owing to the target restrictions.

Other arguments against such an attack would include the difficulty of unobtrusively drilling the necessary shaft; however ingeniously camouflaged, a full-sized drilling rig established near a volcano in a foreign country is liable to cause comment, to say the least. A more restrained approach might involve submarine drilling, with the myriad problems of underwater work (most volcanic areas are near the sea). Alternatively, a subdued and speculative variaton of this approach would be to place massive conventional bombs in the hope of encouraging the seepage of water into the magma (and in the hope that the explosions would be thought of as preliminary tremors associated with the eruption – which they would be, of course). The obvious way is to set off a thermonuclear bomb in the actual crater; this might just be considered as a drastic and spectscular show of force in the nuclear 'chicken' game, but the main point of fiddling about with 'natural' volcanic forces would be to *avoid* nuclear use – and perhaps even overt acts of war – while harassing the enemy as best one may. Nuclear use is not subtle.

II: Fault Finding

The strong-based promontory
Have I made shake, and by the spurs pluck'd up
The pine and cedar —
SHAKESPEARE, The Tempest

As the huge plates which make up Earth's crust grind past one another, or meet with titanic buckling and the forcing of one down, one up, there is a constant building-up of stress which is regularly released in tremors of the ground or in full-scale earthquakes. On average there are something like a million earthquakes of all intensities in a year; of these, a hundred or so are likely to be serious; of the hundred, perhaps ten will be catastrophic. A classic earthquake was recorded in 1755: although the quake's origin was underwater and some distance away, the effect on Lisbon was disastrous. Three successive shocks pulverised the houses in the lower part of the town, and were felt thousands of kilometres away. The sea retreated to an abnormal distance and then rolled back in a 12-metre tidal wave to complete the destruction: some 60,000 people died. In the absence of tidal waves, earthquakes are often followed by immensely destructive fires as in the San Francisco quake of 1908 – gas mains and electric cables were fractured, domestic fires and industrial furnaces overturned. (San Francisco, as it happens, tended to suffer fires even without the excuse of an earthquake.) Fires added greatly to the deaths in the Japanese quake of 1923 (over 140,000 deaths); older disasters were still more lethal if the figures can be trusted, with 200,000 Japanese deaths in 1703, 300,000 Indian ones in 1737 and well over 800,000 in the northern Chinese quake of 1556.

Earthquakes, in fact, involve the release of considerably *more* energy than nuclear weapons; the evil effects are greatly reduced by the wide area over which the energy is spread, and the more gradual rate of its release. The huge killer earthquakes may have a total energy release equivalent to thousands of megatons of TNT, but this is all shockwave and dissipates itself in the attempt to move the immense bulk of the Earth itself. (A bullet will rip fatally through a man; fired at a sandbag, it dissipates its energy harmlessly and even if the bag hangs freely it will swing only slowly.) Nuclear weapons kill through heat-flash, blast, radiation; an earthquake never has the *concentration* of energy in one place to produce a blast-wave in the air. Instead the whole Earth can be set ringing like a monstrous gong of low, low note (to be measured in cycles per hour). The vibrations are obviously strongest near the earthquake's focus; when they take place on the sea-bed the effects can be particularly disastrous, for huge masses of water are set into resonant motion, often spilling over into gigantic tsunamis (mis-called 'tidal waves') on the continental shelves. A 30-metre tsunami may be far more destructive than the shock of the actual quake.

The triggering of an earthquake might therefore be a very useful achievement in warlike terms. Where one zone of the crust is acted upon by forces which make it scrape past another, it may do so gradually or it may stick; in the latter case, stress builds up and can eventually be released in a sudden motion, as an earthquake. Control of earthquakes has been suggested – for example, by pumping liquids into surface faults in order to lubricate the earth-masses and reduce the friction so that they slip past one another steadily and stress build-ups are discouraged. This approach may be disastrous in cases where high levels of stress already exist – the effect may be to trigger an earthquake rather than prevent one. The same effect can be seen in microcosm by simply pressing one's hand against a smooth surface and trying to move it along: on a surface such as glass or ice the hand slides gradually along, while on rough wood it sticks through friction until the force applied has built up to the point where the hand slips suddenly and catastrophically. Applying oil to the wood before starting will make it slippery, prevent the disaster; apply oil when great force is already present between hand and wood, and the disaster is merely hastened.

An alternative means of earthquake-generation would be to give the whole system a kick – to pick a likely earthquake zone like the San Andreas Fault (whose slippages regularly shake California) and administer a small shock with a tactical nuclear device. Provided that there is sufficient accumulated stress, the result should be a made-to-order earthquake; of course, if this trick is attempted too soon after a 'real', a natural, quake, there will have been no time for stresses to build up and the results will be negligible. Here, then, is a means of triggering quakes – which once again crosses the nuclear threshold; it is extremely unlikely that the effect could be achieved with conventional explosive, while the laborious business of pumping lubricants into faults is by no means guaranteed reliable and in any case will be impracticable on hostile soil. Even in a nuclear war, there is little hope for the idea of amplifying nuclear strikes by using them to trigger quakes rather than for direct destruction. Although people may happily go on living in known earthquake zones (which generally include the active volcanic zones, but are far more extensive – even the UK suffers minor quakes, with such dire effects as the falling stone which in the London of 1580 killed one apprentice) with no less enthusiasm than the farmers who till the lower slopes of Vesuvius, military planners are notoriously more hardheaded when placing sites. There are possible exceptions resulting from overwhelming strategic considerations or from simple error – to take an unclassified case, the Diablo Canyon nuclear power station in California turned out to be within three kilometres of an active fault – but the vast majority of missile silos and other strategic installations are far away from danger areas.

To summarise: the obvious means of turning the enemy's own territory against him, so to speak, don't seem especially useful. Harassment could be caused by use of some fearful and as yet undiscovered 'earthquake ray' which might trigger earthquakes and raise volcanoes at vast distances; even if military damage were not done, the effect would be a means of distracting enemy attention – creating a diversion at some crucial moment. In a touchy diplomatic crisis one might gain a few days' breathing-space with the aid of a good disaster on enemy soil . . . About the 'earthquake ray' we can only speculate. Perhaps the secret might be to consider the Earth as a lens through which quake vibrations pass; perhaps a battery of nuclear mines, correctly timed and placed (underground in friendly lands), might generate a shockwave which the great lens of the Earth could focus to the desired point.

One aspect of earthquake devastation does suggest a genuine military point. Tsunami destruction can cause the greater part of damage from a quake or volcanic explosion; and a multimegaton nuclear weapon, if exploded under-water, can give rise to tremendous waves. This suggests two possibilities, neither of them reassuring; in each case advantage may be taken of the fact that many important cities – London, New York – are highly vulnerable to the onslaught of great waves. The frame of mind which welcomes the neutron bomb as a property-sparing destroyer of life may likewise welcome the chance of drowning without smashing a city; if some thought were spared for the possibility of occupation after the nuclear war of attrition, just such measures might be employed. Secondly, this form of attack represents a fine nuance – a 'sub-rung' on Kahn's ladder. All-out nuclear war might be fought in a rapid flurry of pre-emptive strike/second strike/mopping-up over the space of a few hours – or it might shift into low gear as each antagonist attempts to outbluff the other in a slow-motion 'chicken' game, missile for missile, airfield for airfield, city for city, rung by rung up the ladder. A nuclear tsunami is effectively a counter-city weapon representing a very high level of escalation, yet no bomb is actually dropped on a city. This sophistry may confuse the issue of retaliation and leave its instigator with a tiny edge in the continuing war of resolution; or, of course, it may not.

III: Downward to the Earth

The fire, the fire is falling!
BLAKE, *The Marriage of Heaven & Hell*

Yet another class of incredibly violent natural cataclysms is the impressive array of Things From Out There. Tons of meteoric material fall to Earth each year in a continuous dustfall, just as the world-wide grumbling of volcanoes and shifting of faults never wholly ceases; but really spectacular and destructive meteor-strikes are as rare as Krakatoa-scale eruptions. The classic case here is the tremendous rock which smashed into Siberia in 1908, a fireball with a blazing ionisation-trail across the sky and impact energy to rival a nuclear explosion. Estimates of the actual explosive force depend on how the evidence is interpreted, and vary from many kilotons to 30 megatons. Close on 2000 square kilometres of forest were flattened, the tree-trunks snapped like matchsticks by the blast wave, while men 60 kilometres distant were bounced into the air as the ground shook. A city struck by such a meteorite would have been erased. So huge was the devastation that it stimulated exotic theories of the meteor's nature – anti-matter? a black hole? a nuclear-powered alien spacecraft? Certainly it is difficult to comprehend the energy acquired by a reasonably massive body as it falls from infinity through the Earth's gravitational field. A body must attain a velocity of 40,000 kph to escape from Earth without further acceleration; conversely, if air resistance is neglected for the moment, a falling body will be accelerated to this speed by gravity – in addition to its original velocity towards Earth. A mass of one ton will have KE equivalent to the explosion of about 15 tons of TNT by the time it reaches the ground. Thus, to achieve a meteoric energy of 30 megatons, a rock of mass 2 million tons must fall. This sounds very large, but a spherical rock less than 120 metres across would serve; the mass of the Great Pyramid of Khufu is some 5 million tons, and this huge structure would have an impact energy of over 70 megatons in the unlikely event of its being dropped to Earth from a great height. In practice this would be reduced by the fact that some portion of its mass would be vaporised on passage through the atmosphere, while air resistance would also reduce the impact velocity, draining off energy into heat which ionises the air. Also a higher proportion of the energy will be absorbed by the ground than in a nuclear explosion of comparable megatonnage.

Naturally we need not fear that even the most extravagant superpower will consider lifting such masses into orbit and beyond. A very rough rule-of-thumb for lifting things off Earth is that is takes two tons of fuel to lift a kilogram of payload out of our 'gravity well'. So a mass sufficient to cause a 1-megaton explosion on re-entry – say 67,000 tons – would need around 150 million tons of fuel to put it in position. Such a procedure is, essentially, a means of storing chemical energy (from the fuel) as gravitational PE (acquired by the rock); but the efficiency of conversion is so low that it's not worthwhile. Nor is a 150-million-ton rocket particularly practical. This inefficiency could lessen as space technology becomes more refined; the *actual* energy required to move a mass of one kilogram from Earth's surface to infinity is about that required to power a 2-kilowatt domestic heater for eight hours, at a UK cost of perhaps 50 pence. Obviously, in this ideally efficient case, there's no need for a ton of fuel.

Other problems of a meteoric weapon include, as always, the atmosphere. Of the steady rain of matter which falls daily from space, the greater part never reaches the ground; atmospheric friction flashes each particle into vapour. The KE acquired by the micrometeors in their long fall is dissipated high above Earth in a push against air-resistance. The startling energies involved are illustrated by the actual, estimated masses; a meteor whose initial mass is only a few milligrams will emit enough energy to be quite visible from Earth – brighter than many stars. The majority of meteoric material falls invisibly as dust (many thousands of tons each year); small masses from milligrams to grams will appear as the traditional 'shooting stars', but rather greater masses are needed to ensure that the meteor reaches Earth. Even very large meteors may suffer from the heating and split as they fall into a shower of smaller pieces, more easily slowed by friction. The whole leaves an ionisation-path through the atmosphere which emits radiations of all frequencies up to and even including X-rays – TV pictures have been blacked out by the emission from meteor-trails.

Another factor which has been suggested to explain the more violent meteor explosions (e.g., Siberia) is the theoretical possibility of fusion triggering. The falling body might, for example, be the head of a small comet containing liquid helium and other frozen gases including hydrogen. (Helium cannot be frozen even by human methods, which produce temperatures within millionths of a degree of absolute zero at $-273.15°C$; owing to starlight and cosmic radiations, bodies in space never become this cold.) Then the tremendous heating as the meteor falls *may* superheat these gases, which *may* be confined by the bulk of the comet's stony body so that they are forced to fuse; or, less improbably, the gigantic shock of impact may super-compress such trapped gases to set off the fusion reaction. It is in fact generally accepted that the Siberian explosion was caused by a comet exploding at some 10 km height; the fusion theory is more speculative. If a rock were deliberately pushed over the brink of Earth's gravity well, and set crashing down upon a city, aggressors might think it worthwhile to sink a deep shaft beforehand and slip in a few drums of lithium deuteride to add to the fun. 'After all,' one imagines them saying, 'It can't do any harm . . .' – unless nuclear use, even of this 'clean' variety, remains taboo.

The advantage of an artificial meteor, whether boosted in this dubious fashion or not, is that as a weapon it could be practically unstoppable. When a massive rock begins to fall from on high, there are *in principle* various ways of preventing it from causing destruction. Firstly, a decelera-ting force might be applied to slow it down, halt, or even reverse its motion – this poses immense practical problems since, even on the ground where we can bring all our forces to bear, mankind finds it impracticable to shift even a small mountain except in a slow-motion, piecemeal fashion which would be useless against a mountain falling with steadily increasing velocity. The only feasible approach would be to fire a flight of nuclear missiles; even these could not hope to push the meteor back into space, but if they were all exploded at one side of it the effect could be to divert the still-falling rock to a wasteland, or at least to shift its impact point far enough from the original target to reduce the devastation. There are several drawbacks to such an approach. Since the country under attack will presumably not know the mass of the incoming meteor, it would be difficult to estimate the required explosive force to divert it, or the likely amount by which it will be diverted after a given force is applied. There is, moreover, the risk of breaking the meteor up into a shower whose wider spread could result in more total damage than the single expected impact; this would probably nullify the highly speculative fusion suggested above, but has little else to commend it unless the attack could be made early enough in the fall that the fragments were largely consumed by frictional heating. And the use of nuclear weapons would add to the frightfulness of the catastrophe by making the meteor itself partly radioactive, in addition to the inevitable fallout.

The most complete way of countering a falling rock, especially if it could be intercepted at a great height, would be a saturation attack with nuclear weapons, sufficient to smash the rock utterly. If it is reduced to tiny pieces its bulk will flash away in the continuing fall and provide little more than a spectacular fireworks display (although the fall-out would remain a problem). Again, the success of this manoeuvre would depend largely on the initial size of the rock. Probably a rock small enough to be completely fragmented by a nuclear weapon would also be too small to do damage on the city-smashing scale; and there are considerable difficulties in arranging a multiple nuclear strike. The missiles would have to be timed to avoid neutralising one another, and their courses corrected to account for whatever change of course the previous strike may have made to the meteor. Any defence of this sort is likely to be a gamble, in which the defender accepts the assured evil of fall-out in exchange for the not-too-great chance that the falling mountain will be scattered harmlessly and that the large pieces, thrown at random about the sky, will not cause worse disaster. Additional problems are posed by the fact that interception systems are not presently geared to precision hitting. A near miss will normally knock out fragile components of an incoming missile, and deactivate the whole thing; but a mass of rock has no weak points in that sense.

Other means of defence tend to require 'engineer's dream' devices. Some form of energy converter whereby the energy of the falling rock simply charges up immense banks of batteries? A perfectly elastic substance to bounce it (like a hard-rubber 'superball') back into the air? A disintegrating ray . . . but lasers have such great difficulty in punching through air and melting a few pounds of metal that the vaporisation of many tons of rock seems virtually impossible.

The problems of defence may be great, but so are those of attack. We have already dismissed as absurd, for the foreseeable future, the possibility of lifting sufficient mass into orbit to provide the material for such a meteoroid (it will be called a meteoroid until it begins to fall through the atmosphere, where it has its brief blaze of glory as a meteor proper; any remnant or remnants found on Earth after the final impact will join the ever-growing class of meteorites). The supply of raw materials will probably be a dominant long-term problem of any major work in space, making it particularly difficult to assemble a weapon which relies upon its sheer mass. Eliminating Earth as a source of supply for reasons of practical economics, the major possibilities are the Moon and the asteroids.

With the technology of the not-too-distant future, it's reasonable to assume that people could travel out to the asteroids, those genuine flying mountains which are thinly scattered between the orbits of Mars and Jupiter. As in the 400,000 km hop to the Moon, most of the expense will go to fight free of the Earth's numbing gravity; a jaunt of a few hundred million kilometres to the asteroids need cost no more than one to the Moon, although, unless more energy were expended to increase the vessel's speed, it would also take several hundred times as long. There is also the question of finding an asteroid at the other end; the average asteroid is an undistinguished chunk of rock less than a kilometre across and separated by (again on average) 15 million kilometres or so from the neighbouring rock. Perhaps in the more overcrowded regions of the asteroid belt this separation will be as little as a million and a half kilometres, a mere four times the distance from Earth to Moon. It would be an extremely lucky asteroid probe which did not slip straight through to the orbit of Jupiter without a single encounter; comets pass in and out of the 'deadly' zone (often pictured as a Sargasso Sea of drifting, menacing rocks through which future spaceships must thread a tortuous path) and no collisions have been recorded.

When the perfect rock has been found, it must be brought back to Earth; and this is where the figures become appalling. Assuming that the rock must be shifted 300 million kilometres from the depths of the asteroid belt, a brief calculation shows that its journey will take a little less than a year if its average velocity is 40,000 kph. The time-lag is sufficiently depressing, but the familiar figure of 40,000 kph is more so; this is about equal to terrestrial escape velocity, and likewise to the theoretical velocity attained by the rock after it has plunged down the precipitous slope of Earth's gravity. Just as the falling rock seems unstoppable, so the distant, stably orbiting one seems at first glance unstartable; anyone wishing to send it crashing down on Earth within a year must apply to it as much energy (to reach that 40,000 kph) as its impact is likely to release (not to mention the problem of cancelling its original orbital speed!). Sufficient chemical fuel to accelerate a few million tons of rock would be prohibitively expensive and difficult to deliver to this remote asteroid; a series of nuclear blasts might do the trick but without much fine control, besides which there would be the continuing risk of causing the rock to break up. The course-correction problems can also be imagined; with such an unweildy projectile it will be hard enough to hit the Earth, let alone a specific target upon its surface.

But we do not need to travel hundreds of millions of kilometres to collect a likely rock. There are a number of rocks, mostly discovered in this century, whose eccentric natural orbits bring them uncomfortably close to Earth as it is. One, Eros, comes within 22 million kilometres; another, Icarus, within 6·5 million kilometres; the predicted orbit of Hermes should have brought it to within a few hundred thousand kilometres – closer than the Moon – but somewhere Out There its course was presumably diverted (e.g., by a close approach to Jupiter) and after that first sighting it failed to reappear. If a close approach does take place, it may be feasible to crack off a portion of one of these mini-planets by means of well-placed nuclear mines, and to steer it over a period of weeks or months far enough into Earth's gravity to set it irretrievably falling. Again, there are objections. Since astronomers take a peculiar interest in these errant bodies (not surprising, with the risk of an accidental collision always present) it would be difficult to split off a piece without the tell-tale nuclear flashes alerting watchers below. Also, with the relatively small distances involved, there is less time for correction of mistakes; if the initial splitting-off goes awry, the aggressors may suffer the painful irony of 'their' rock falling inexorably towards their own country. After such consideration of falling masses as weapons, the irony would be still greater should even one of the smaller wandering rocks (like Apollo, Iarus, Adonis) strike Earth through natural causes. Their masses are to be measured in many thousands of millions of tons, rather than the puny millions so far discussed; such an impact could wipe out entire continents.

In the absence of asteroids, the most practical source of material is the Moon. Very much less work need be don to lift large masses from its surface; the escape velocity is only 8,500 kph as compared with 40,000 kph for the Earth, and the 'escaoe energy' for a given mass is proportional to the *square* of this velocity (by the kinetic energy formula: $KE = \frac{1}{2}mv^2$). Thus, if the theoretical cost in terms of electrical power of lifting a one-kilogram mass free of the Earth is 50p (90 cents), for the Moon it would only be slightly more than 1p (2 cents). And conditions are such that we can come closer to this theoretical ideal on the Moon; for one thing, there is no atmosphere to speak of, so it becomes practicable to boost something to escape velocity quite near the lunar surface and allow it to fly away (on Earth, air-friction would make this approach prohibitively expensive – not to mention the noise problems of actual motion at 40,000 kph or Mach 33!). This very situation forms part of the plot in Heinlein's novel *The Moon is a Harsh Mistress*, where Earth is bombarded from the Moon by large – precise mass unspecified – rocks launched by means of a 'catapult' or linear motor on the Moon's surface.

Professor Gerard O'Neill, advocate of space colonisation, has given much consideration to such a catapult, which he calls a mass driver, in the hope that it could be used to supply free-falling colonies from the Moon. Essentially the device consists of a series of electromagnet coils arranged along a tube; the 'ammunition', or payload, is magnetically suspended within this tube, and timed electrical pulses are applied to the coils so that as the payload travels along the tube it receives a series of pulses, each accelerating it a little more until it flies from the end at high speed. O'Neill's first model accelerated its load to 135 kph in one-tenth of a second; his proposed lunar version would be about 15 kilometres long and would accelerate much larger loads to above lunar escape velocity in about 8 seconds. The efficiency could be as great as 97%. The *direction* of escape is not important when there's no atmosphere to slow the payload; provided its course does not immediately hit mountains, etc., any mass travelling at more than escape velocity will never return to the Moon. O'Neill suggests that his lunar catapult would be able to push 50,000 tons of material into space each month: Heinlein's fictional catapult is similar but apparently able to handle larger individual loads. In theory, precise timing and acceleration should be able to drop a rock practically anywhere on Earth from a Moon-based catapult; an infinite number of possible trajectories are available, from near-straight lines to wide, lazy curves which would take many months to negotiate. In practice, some means of making minor course corrections will also be necessary. Perhaps a catapult would suffer from limitations in the mass of its missiles – hundreds of tons rather than thousands or millions – but this might be remedied by launching large numbers of them. the missiles themselves could be just plain lunar rock, either jacketed with steel to provide magnetic 'grip' (Heinlein) or launched from magnetic 'buckets' which eject their payload and remain below (O'Neill).

An objection to this approach is that the catapult (which of course would normally be used for peaceful purposes) is excessively vulnerable; the location of a device kilometres long is difficult to conceal, and only a small section of the accelerator track need be knocked out to make it useless. Heinlein suggests building underground, though without much real conviction; the true advantage could be the ability to make many launches which might be 'unstoppably' on their way long before missiles from Earth could arrive to retaliate. The gravity well which sucks in the falling rocks will drag like quicksand at the missiles as they rise. Perhaps the country controlling the catapult might interrupt its peaceful business, just briefly, to toss a single rock on its way towards a major enemy city. A natural disaster? The enemy might have his suspicions, but it could be hard to be quite sure . . . Such an isolated attack might be useful as a diversion or distraction, or perhaps even a means for A (controlling the catapult) to provoke war between B and C when they are not on good terms.

If the catapult *is* controlled by a single nation, it provides the ultimate second-strike capability. Any heavy entrenchment of weapons on the Moon will have this effect; it may take time for them to be deployed, but enemy missiles struggling 'uphill' can be detected in plenty of time. Even if they cannot be neutralised, the wave of rocks, missiles or whatever from the Moon can be started on its way before anything can happen to the catapult. Of course, even if nation A has the only catapult, B and C may set up armed bases on the Moon for the sole purpose of taking out A's catapult in the event of war. And A will try to develop the capability to eliminate such bases before his catapult can suffer – and B may build a catapult of his own – and, in the long run, the shifting of weaponry off Earth (at present forbidden by treaty, at least where 'nukes' are concerned) could lead to situations as messy and complex as today's.

A genuine meteor of city-smashing size falls from time to time . . . the Siberia bolides of 1908 and 1947 may be the only ones of this century, but there is no way of telling.

These small bodies, of the order of a kilometre across, must come very close to Earth before they can be detected. There was a near-miss in 1972 which took everyone by surprise – a fireball which whizzed over North America less than 60 kilometres up and vanished back into space. Had it fallen to the ground, it is estimated that, although it was a small body – perhaps 12 metres in diameter – the result would have been a Hiroshima-size explosion. It might be sensible to concentrate some effort on remote detection of such intruders (Arthur C. Clarke's SPACEGUARD project) in the hope that something salutary and nuclear could be done about a dangerously-aimed rock; but the sensible action has always tended to elude mankind.

CHAPTER SIX

NEW ARSENALS

I: EcoWar Revisited

Wanted: mad geneticist with experience in recombinant DNA research, to form part of a team investigating new virus particles with a view to world domination. Salary will be on a profit-sharing basis; it is expected to be low at first, but rising within a year or two (dependent on satisfactory results) to around £10 million p.a., with annual increments thereafter as nation after nation capitulates to our demands ...

NOTICEBOARD ANNOUNCEMENT AT THE
UNIVERSITY OF ASTON

Biological warfare has a long and dishonourable history behind it, stretching back to the mucky weapons mentioned in Chapter 1, and to the old stratagems of tossing a very dead horse into the waterhole the enemy may be expected to use, or into the town where he's besieged. Plagues may now be spread in slightly more sophisticated ways with specially bred bacteria or viruses, but there remains the problem of controlling the spread. Such a means of killing may thus appeal only to terrorist groups, blackmailers (as at the head of this chapter) and – in general – those either indifferent to their own safety or able to protect themselves (a small group might hide behind sanitary barriers; an entire population cannot). There is much less difficulty in starting the plague than in stopping it. Yet, in its way, disease can theoretically be a *precision* weapon on the large or statistical scale; as a high-velocity rifle offers precision in individual deaths, a well-documented virus could operate with hideous impartiality to eliminate 10%, or 20%, or 50%, of its victims, inflicting a predetermined amount of damage on the enemy. 100% lethality, although unlikely, is unnecessary if the wish is to smash a society.

A disease is made lethal through unfamiliarity – if it can take the body's immune systems by surprise, the danger is increased. 'Trivial' childhood diseases of Western civilisations, like measles, can be fatal plagues in societies without a history of infection and acclimatisation. Smallpox has been virtually eradicated from the Earth; if it were to emerge once more after long absence, the consequences might be terrible until fresh vaccines could be manufactured – and vaccination is no cure, but a preventive means of stimulating the body's defence systems into increased resistance to a specific disease. It has thus been suggested that, like any other threatened species, the smallpox virus should be preserved from extinction – just in case. Certainly someone, somewhere may be preserving the disease for less than noble reasons. Antibiotics like penicillin and the rest can attack a disease directly, but there is a *Catch-22* type problem associated with their widespread use: an antibiotic will remain effective against bacteria until over-used. This is a clear example of Darwinian natural selection. If all the bacteria of a given disease were the same, each would succumb to a given concentration of a given antibiotic. However, in each generation (and bacteria can go through many generations in an hour) there will be a scattering of mutants; the complete plans for producing a new bacterium are stored in coils of nucleic acid (DNA) in the genes of each member of the previous generation, and once in a while these plans include a 'misprint'.

DNA, for all its mystery and complexity, *is* just a chemical compound – a chain of amino acids; it can be changed like any other compound. A gross change 'kills' it and makes it unable to take part in reproduction; a minor change means an alteration in the genetic message carried. There are mutagenic chemicals which distort portions of the DNA chain or lock on to it to cause the 'misprints'; radiation can disrupt the links or even transmute the elements of which they are composed; and in the next generation the mutations appear. Some of the changed bacteria are incapable of life; others are weakened by the alteration and succumb more easily; still more have irrelevant features which make them neither happier nor sadder bacteria; and a very few may actually prove more resistant to antibiotic X, the standard remedy for the disease they cause. Refrain from using antibiotic X and the disease may run its course unhindered; use it, and natural selection comes into play, for the more resistant bacteria will be a little less affected and will increase their numbers relative to the rest. As the disease goes on from person to person and is treated each time with X, the tougher bacteria come to dominate the population, and also undergo further mutations . . . some of which may eventually produce a breed that is tougher still. On each successive patient, the antibiotic X treatment is a little less effective, and presently it is useless. Perhaps now the disease can only be attacked by switching to antibiotic Y, which ironically might have had no effect on the original strain of bacteria.

This slow evolutionary process may just as well be carried out in a culture-dish with the specific intention of breeding super-bacteria; and this has been done. Since now we are developing the capability to interfere *directly* with the DNA programme through 'genetic engineering' (physically by micro-surgical transplantation of genetic material, biologically by the use of viruses which attack and alter the nucleic-acid chains), more efficient and ingenious diseases may well be in the offing. One can imagine the

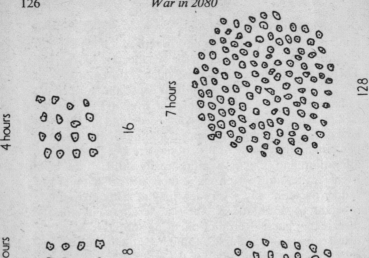

Fig. 4 Runaway growth: if bacteria divide each hour, a single mutant can give rise to up to 2^{24} (nearly 17,000,000) individuals in a day.

possibility of a 'self-destruct' virus whose potency is programmed to decrease over many generations, so that after wiping out half a population it sinks into harmlessness. Or perhaps a virus with a secret weakness: although seemingly invulnerable and deadly, its very structure incorporates a 'keyhole' into which some innocuous compound known only to the makers will fit, to break up the virus or render it harmless. Or, nastiest of all, a racist disease: however much the intellectual difference between races is disputed and made the subject of pointless argument, physical differences do certainly exist. A tailor-made virus might selectively attack one group, whether whites or blacks or browns or yellows, and leave the rest unscathed. The key-in-the-lock principle could activate rather than neutralise an apparently harmless virus, which might switch to its killing form at the touch of some specific substance in the bloodstream – aspirins following a headache, various hormones in the bloodstream following anger or sexual desire, or even simple compounds like alcohol. The deadliness of these variegated diseases must also be carefully controlled, so that each victim may infect many more before his collapse.

But all these unpleasant thoughts are for the confines of the ivory tower. A toilored virus might operate reliably in the laboratory; out in the wide world, exposed in vast numbers to mutagens and radiation, the viruses may evolve unpredictably. In particular, they may no longer be susceptible to the built-in means of control suggested above. Once differences have become established in a virus population, application of control will accentuate them just as antiobiotics breed resistant micro-organisms. Along all the roads of war with disease stand warning signs inscribed *Danger* and *Here be random variables;* here above all is where one's own weapons are more to be feared than the enemy's.

This dread backlash may be avoided, in part at least, by warring not against the enemy but against his crops. If his principle vegetable is the turnip, then a turnip-specific virus will damage him more than it could an aggressor in whose economy turnips played no part. Virus mutations would be of less consequence, there being no selection-pressure forcing the virus to make the (difficult) leap to another species of vegetable; it may rage unchecked among the turnips for all the aggressors care.

Of course there are easier ways of assaulting an ecological system. If the introduction of the rabbit to Australia had been planned as an act of war, it would have been one of the great coups of history; it is sobering to think that somewhere on Earth – or somewhere in a future laboratory – there may lurk an innocuous insect which would run amok in just such a fashion in Asia, Europe, America. Virtually unstoppable pests have already emerged, like Dutch Elm Disease (fortunately elms are not vital to anyone's economy) or the water-hyacinth which chokes canals with incredible speed, or the brown rat (which at least had the virtue in the UK of displacing the old black rat, carrier of the Great Plague). Again one would choose a pest which preyed enthusiastically on enemy turnips while sparing one's own potatoes; perhaps a little genetic tinkering might make the pest still more of a pest. In general, the larger the animal the less frequent the generations; bacteria and insects (like the ubiquitous *Drosophila* fruit-flies of genetics) can be studied and tinkered with through many generations in the laboratory, while a breed of deadly rogue elephants (gestation period 18 months) could not be produced on the same timescale.

Physical (as opposed to biological) methods of interfering with an ecology tend to be a little more obvious. the tons upon tons of defoliants dropped on Vietnam may have been effective in a limited way (although jungle recovers swiftly) but they were neither subtle nor unobtrusive. Similarly, one might consider gigantic mirrors in orbit. made from superlight aluminised plastic, which would direct the Sun's rays to increase the temperature of a certain area and wreck the climate and crops; but it doesn't seem likely that this could be done covertly. It is at best an inefficient means for a very large country to oppress a very small one. In the same way, a small country could be deprived of rainfall by industrious seeding of clouds *before* they reached it; this could be more covert, but not for long! The same goes for the spraying of lakes with oil to reduce evaporation and hence the rainfall of neighbours down-wind. Climate control in general offers itself as an interesting means of waging war, or at least of harassing the enemy – interesting but apparently not efficient. There are more widespread possibilities such as an artificially increased 'greenhouse effect' in which CO_2, etc., in the atmosphere leads to increased retention of solar heat, following which the polar icecaps melt and flood half the world. The converse is an effect whereby clouds of pollutants increase the reflectivity (albedo) of Earth and by turning away more sunlight precipitate a new Ice Age. These are manifestly indiscriminate weapons, if they are weapons at all; control of such effects is a weapon against whole planets and not to be used in conflicts of nation against nation.

A technology, like an ecology, has its vital areas and its weak points. We might do better to consider subtle means of attacking these. The natural selection process already discussed may possibly evolve bacteria which can attack a greater variety of dead materials – like the plastic-eating bacteria which have been suggested as a means of recycling waste plastics. In theory, one simply maintains a bacteria-culture on minimal 'food' plus plenty of minced polythene; if a mutant able to metabolise the plastic should develop it will do better than the rest, having more to eat. This is grossly oversimplified; it may be necessary to resort to genetic tampering before a plastic-eater could be developed, but the effects of one could obviously be catastrophic. If polythene or PVC could be metabolised, there are other, less tightly-bonded organic compounds which might prove even more nutritious – TNT, for example, and plastic explosive. Something which *only* ate these things might be a little difficult to spread – one cannot go to the trouble of separately infecting each enemy magazine – so the ideal explosive-eater would be carried in the human body, able to eke out an existence there, and would be harmless but contagious. Then, at the breath of each infected worker, the explosive triggers of H-bombs would begin gradually to fester and decay . . .

The fertile imaginations of science-fiction writers have of course produced many exciting diseases which may cause one (in H. P. Lovecraft's immortal words) to 'disintegrate into an abhorrent plasticity of fungous loathesomeness', or to be converted cell by cell to plastic (which merely sounds a little silly) as in Hodder-Williams's *The Prayer Machine* – or a hundred other interesting symptoms which obscure the prime purpose of a weapon, which is to kill people. Bio-warfare researchers presumably do not say to each other such things as: 'Look, Dr Jackson! If I tie in another ketone group *there* the victims will drip green slime!'. Of course, it may be that diseases which merely reduce efficiency could be spread; an army of men suffering from severe hay-fever will not be fighting at its best. If there is no story in science fiction which explains how the common cold is the softening-up weapon of some alien invasion, it's about time somebody wrote it.

II: We Have the Technology –

I teach you the Superman. Man is something that is to be surpassed.
NIETZCHE, *Thus Spake Zarathustra*

This chapter has begun among the warlike possibilities of biology, and will conclude with the more familiar matters of engineering and physics; but in between we should pause to consider the interdisciplinary matters: what has been called the marriage of flesh and machine. Probes have already been sent from various directions into this debatable territory . . . the old notion of using birds as vectors for disease (which like all plague weapons cuts both ways) gives place to that of the trained dolphin which carries bombs towards undersea targets, or in a more advanced version has the bomb stitched intimately into its body. Men and women who are part machine are already around in thousands, with plastic arteries, steel bones, electronic heart-pacemakers, electromechanical hands and whole workshops full of other wonders; there is no reason why – say for assassination purposes – suitable charges of plastic explosive should not be built into a suicide volunteer, to be detonated voluntarily, or into an unknowing victim for detonation by remote control. Meanwhile, the planners of 'intelligent' mechanical systems think hungrily of the human eyes and brain, with a pattern-recognition capability superior to any machine yet built; if only they could be *borrowed* for the otherwise adequate machine!

The 'mechanical cyborg', the man (or woman, but I'll skip the unwieldiness of continually saying 'he or she', 'his or her', etc.) who for health reasons has had artificial bits added to his body, is naturally created for no other reason than to restore his functioning as a human being – to make him normal. To make a man a better weapon he must be made in some way super-normal: in science fiction this covers a vast spectrum, from the hero of Frederic Brown's *Rogue in Space*, who has a weighted artificial hand with which he hits people, to the prosthetic-armed villain of Samuel Delany's *Nova*, whose new improved fingers can crush and fuse sand until it becomes glass (this was a favourite trick of Superman's although he thriftily preferred to squeeze fragments of coal into diamonds). The same fantasy of overcompensation, whereby the deficient becomes the superior, is to be found in TV's 'bionic' people – for example, the man who wrenches open steel doors with his electro-mechanical replacement arm, while being mysteriously able to brace himself against the jamb with his other, merely human, arm. In the same way his lady colleague lifts cars in her artificial arms while standing on her artificial legs; her spine, although unmodified, fails to collapse beneath the strain. This illustrates the need to think things through, and the fact that the human body is far more weak and vulnerable than any mechanical aids which may be built into it. In a way, it is also not *big* enough to be protected by mere modification; despite the experiences of various 'invulnerable' comic-book heroes, even the ability to withstand a nuclear explosion does not exempt one from the laws of action and reaction, as a result of which the blast is liable to throw said heroes hundreds of kilometres, if not completely clear of the planet. An adapted man is not likely to be of very much use as a fighter in a battlefield of machines; to become an efficient war machine he will probably have to give up being a man.

Minor improvements have been made to the body in the course of surgery intended to make it more normal. Bones of stainless titanium-steel are very obviously tougher than those provided by nature; a man whose skeleton is entirely replaced by metal would be very much more resistant to fractures. He would also be heavier and slowed in his movements, since it's difficult to produce artificial bones which are both strong and have the lightness of the real thing. In addition, a steel-boned man would very soon be dead – unless he were given blood-tranfusions every few hours, or unless blood-producing marrow could be persuaded to grow in the artificial bones. A human modification which actually had some military value turned up in the earlier days of eye surgery, when plastic lenses were grafted into defective eyes. It seems that these lenses differed from the real thing – and from ordinary glass – in that they transmitted light at higher frequencies in the near ultraviolet, by definition invisible. The retina reacts to UV, although the lens normally blocks it. In World War II a few such people fortuitously able to see UV were used as coastal watchers – a precaution against spies who signalled in 'black light'.

This is the general level of improvements to the human body itself: interesting and of specialist use, but not of vital importance. A few other possible modifications follow . . . Built-in armour – a plastic/metal mesh protection over vital organs, which would make the body more resistant to knives or shrapnel but scarcely less vulnerable to a rifle or bomb – and why not just wear a flak jacket? Electronic telepathy, achieved by implanting integrated-circuit transceivers – excellent for co-ordinating armies, but of little more use than an external transceiver (except perhaps in very noisy environments). The ability to 'plug in' to machines and control them intimately . . . but this is moving away from the prospect of human modification to that of symbiosis with the machine – a wider field where the object is not to make improvements within the limitations of the human form, but to integrate the human power of control into a system which is essentially machine.

These symbiotic systems effectively extend the human range without necessarily modifying the body. A good primitive example is the motor-car; a driver does not think 'I must now slow down – must move my foot on to the brake pedal and push it downwards', he simply sees the need to slow down, which is at once translated into the reflex action of pressing the brake. Driving an automobile can be mastered, intellectually, in a very few minutes; the long grind of training which most of us must undergo is necessary to programme the reflexes so that the automobile becomes an extension of the body. The brain controls its speed and direction without real thought for what the hands and feet are actually doing, any more than a man bending his arm thinks: 'Now I must contract my biceps so as to exert leverage upon the ulna.' He simply *does* it. A good driver becomes the brain and nervous system of his automobile.

It would be still easier to accept as an extension of the body a machine which functions in the same way – one with arms and legs. One such system is called the Walking Truck – a four-legged machine nearly three and a half metres high and weighing well over a ton. The operator is strapped into a sensor system which interprets his body movements: if he pushes forward with one hand, the machine's 'foreleg' pushes in the same way with vastly greater force; if he goes through the motions of crawling, they are interpreted and amplified to make the whole machine lurch along. It may not be feasible for a man to lift immense weights with 'bionic arms', but as a part of this man/machine combination he can lift the weights as though with his own arms. Walking machines ('pedipulators') replace the legendary seven-league boots, enabling the operator to cross rough country in six- or fifteen-metre strides. The ultimate development of this principle could lead to something like the combat suits of Heinlein's *Starship Troopers*, which vastly amplify the force exerted by the man inside – as well as being fitted with radar and other scanners, a wealth of communications gear, miniature jets, rocket-launchers, etc., etc.

These devices are not purely mechanical; their controls involve nothing so simple as the car accelerator, which merely opens and closes a petrol valve. Sophisticated electronics is needed to interpret body movements and convert them to corresponding movements of the machine; in between, the instructions exist only as chains of electrical impulses. These can be transmitted over radio links if necessary; the operator can have equal control and a good deal more safety from a sensor-web perhaps thousands of kilometres away, able to see and hear (and even feel) exactly what his distant mechanical limbs are doing. Such remote operation of mechanical manipulators has been called telefactoring. Sight and hearing are supplied by a TV camera and microphone; touch is provided partly by feedback through the mechanical sensors (which become a little harder to move when a heavy weight is being lifted) and partly through tiny patterns of air-jets at the operator's fingertips, which give more detailed tactile information. Miniature pedipulators could stride on missions of reconnaissance or even attack and sabotage without risk to human life (except those of the unfortunate foemen who are attacked or who succeed in capturing the machine, in which case its master presses the DESTRUCT button . . .). A variant on the intelligent missile is also offered – the man-controlled walking or flying bomb, whose TV eye, relaying data to the man behind, guides it exactly to its target, taking all manner of evasive action without the supposed predictability of a machine.

Other experiments are already being conducted on such

weapons as guns directly linked to the human eye and head; the electromechanical interpreter follows (optically) the movements of the eye, instructing servo-mechanisms to drive a mounted gun so that it points in the same direction. our hero has only to *look* at the target and the gun is aimed; to fire he can press a button or simply raise an eyebrow. there are innumerable means of triggering the gun, of course – it could be done by gritting the teeth, twitching the foot, pressing the knees together, whistling – whatever the designers and the operator find mutually convenient. Ultimately, by wiring transducers directly into the human nervous system, it becomes possible for the human brain to control machinery by nothing but thought. A disembodied brain with suitable life-support could be wired into just about anything – any system requiring detection and action – spotting incoming missiles *via* radar and attacking them with a laser, or looking out from just such a missile taking necessary evasive action. In general, however, such an extreme seems pointless; for the brain there is at present no better life-support system than the body, and so there is no reason to accept a mechanical second-best unless some real advantage is gained. The missile might not be adequate to carry a whole body, for example (in which case it would have trouble with the blood, nutrient and oxygen supplies for a brain); in any case, it appears that micro-computer systems can handle most problems of missile guidance and are steadily improving.

Hanging firmly on to the archiac human body, we can still link men directly with their weapons, as in the various science-fiction stories (Ken Bulmer's *On The Symb-Socket Circuit*, Samuel Delany's *Nova*) where men are fitted with sockets for interconnection with machines. New senses can then be provided *via* the machines – as in the cats which, thanks to miniature Geiger counters which feed their impulses to brain implants are able to sense nuclear radiations. That would be useful for any soldier on a futuristic battlefield; he plugs into his Heinlein-style battle armour, or into the giant tank which he controls as an extension of his body, and his sense of taste (say) is overridden by signals from the radiation detector. While handling the tank literally by feel, aiming and firing the guns by eye and carrying on a voice dialogue with the command post, he *tastes* the radioactive areas of the battlefield, their strength and relative direction, and carefully avoids them . . .

There are thus three ways of running things upon a hyper-technological battlefield. The operator can be in the driver's seat, whether wired-up or simply controlling his war-engine as he might an automobile or a pedipulator. In this case, he is vulnerable. Human minds are cheap to produce, but even the most bloodthirsty general should bow to the economic fact that they are not cheap to train, while the machines they operate are extremely expensive. In addition to his well known vulnerability, a human needs food, drink and a fair amount of space. Cybernetic systems are less vulnerable in some ways – a solid-state computer could theoretically be almost immune to shock. They are more immediately susceptible to radiation flashes, which instantly do unspeakable things to semi-conductors (even nuclear-weapon levels of radiation take over half an hour to affect men); on the other hand, machines can often recover from such damage, although computers may need reprogramming. The real disadvantage of computers as computers, *at present*, is that they do not have the visual recognition ability, nor the judgement, of men.

The telefactor system, where a human safely behind the lines operates a machine by remote controls, should overcome all the problems of human vulnerability and many problems of computers. The human is not even present – he is tucked away beneath many feet of concrete at the command post, although, as far as the battle is concerned, his mind appears to be in the machine to which he is linked by an electro-magnetic umbilical cord. Since the directing intelligence is human, the actual machine does not need computers of great complexity; if momentarily disabled by a radiation burst, the systems can be re-activated almost at once by the human operator. The problem is to maintain the communications link – radio may be jammed, lasers are linked to line-of-sight use, long wires are both vulnerable and rather silly. Perhaps a combination of radio and lasers beamed from satellite links would be most successful; perhaps not. The suitability of telefactor weapons on the open battlefield is very much dependent on back-room conflicts – on whether the communicators or the jammers come up with the more successful systems.

Ultimately there is no reason why the human should not *become* the machine. He could discard his body and somehow transfer his awareness to a data-bank. His new body would be anything he dared to plug in to his electronic nervous system. This may be the only hope of true immortality. In a pure machine environment, anything desired can be conjured up – there is the possibility of tremendous subjective battle and adventure in the tranquillity of computer simulation, with men's senses being fed data just as satisfying as the 'real world' could give their old organs of flesh. It would be Valhalla – a glorious dead end; it could be possible within the next century.

III: The Growth of Hardware

Giants and the genii,
Multiplex of wing and eye,
Whose strong obedience broke the sky
When Solomon was king.

G. K. CHESTERTON, *Lepanto*

As we peer further and further into a murky future, the details of the forces available to mankind become blurred. By the 2080 of this book's title, great changes will have been made even in the energy-sources which power civilisation. Oil and coal will have been supplanted – must have been if high technology is to be maintained – by fusion and perhaps solar power (carried on microwave beams from space?). We cannot now imagine the ultimate forms which fusion-power will take, but we can assume that in its final form it will be cheaper and more efficient than today's fission reactors – not to mention being a good deal 'cleaner'. This, coupled with the further development of the laser, suggests that laser artillery will become possible and perhaps even moderately cheap – overcoming the problems of firing through air by the simple expedient of pumping out vastly more power to compensate for the losses. (An example of a possible system: since fusion produces many neutrons and a laser can demonstrably be pumped by neutrons using a fissile lasing material, a highly efficient laser might be directly coupled to a miniature fusion source if one can be built.) Similarly, mini-accelerators might generate extremely fast particle beams, increasing the ability of electrons or protons to punch through air by taking advantage of relativistic effects: as it approaches the speed of light, the effective mass of a particle is increased;

so at half the speed of light – $0.5c$ – the effective mass of a particle is increased by some 15%, at $0.99c$ it appears to weigh seven times its 'rest mass', and at c itself the mass appears infinite (i.e., one would have to use infinite energy to accelerate a particle to c in our Universe).

With beam weapons of such power available, we can certainly expect to see them extensively deployed as ground-based ballistic-missile defences – in the absence, that is, of international disarmament backed up by imspection parties with access to everything. With a screen of ground-based and satellite-based lasers, it seems certain that the traditional ICBM in all its forms will vanish. Conventional artillery will not necessarily be outmoded by lasers, which cannot be fired except at visible targets – there is no possibility of lobbing beams of light, like shells, over the hills or over the horizon. The device which *does* eliminate old-style artillery is the miniature guided missile. Cruise missiles of the present day can contain enough computer-power to follow a terrain map to arrive within tens of metres of their intended targets; a very little more sophistication and the smaller missiles, which can be carried and launched by an ordinary foot soldier, will be able to hop over a hill, buzz along a few metres above ground level to take advantage of all available cover, weave from side to side and confuse defensive fire, and ultimately explode (unless taken out by a laser) at the precise co-ordinates taken from a satellite map and punched into them by the soldier. Larger and highly 'intelligent' cruise missiles will zig-zag through defences in the same way, succeeding or failing according to the closeness with which defensive lasers are spaced. In theory, when it's laser against missile the laser should win; but perhaps a wave of mirror-surfaced, laser-armed missiles could knock out the defence laser installations so that the nuclear-armed ones could slip through . . .

In time of war, other lasers would be turned permanently upward to dazzle or perhaps destroy the satellite spies. Satellites could become especially vulnerable through their low mass, with the increasing power available to ground-based installations; a satellite firing downward, even with a powerful beam (nuclear-reactor gas laser?), will have to heat up a much larger installation. Perhaps particle beams, which seem to have rather less potential, will overtake lasers in their development and 'particle beam' should be read for 'laser' in much of the above. Neither should microwave beams be forgotten; several present-day scientists suggest that they will make practical power beams for transferring energy from those space-based solar cells, in which case the power beam could itself be made a dangerous weapon (not at the envisaged levels of transmission – but things are not the same in war!). One imagines dead cities of microwave-grilled people.

If all these energies can be tossed about in such a spendthrift fashion, we can at least hope that a 'clean' fusion bomb will have been developed. It might compress its lithium deuteride, or new improved substitute, with the aid of a mini-laser, or of a particle beam, or with some amazingly potent explosive which can be shaped to develop the required shockwave for those vital nanoseconds while the fusion reaction builds up. This bomb would produce the usual fireball, and a blast of neutrons and gamma-rays, and a blast-wave in the air; but there would be no fall-out on the scale produced by fission bombs. What fall-out there was would be from previously stable compounds 'acti-vated' by the neutrons – principally radioactive carbon-14 made from the air's nitrogen in the reaction $N-14 + neutron \rightarrow C-14 + proton$. With such an ultimate development of the neutron bomb in general use, and the laser defences already mentioned, there would be a good chance of picking up the pieces even after nuclear Total War; despicable though it may be to 'kill people and spare property', the notion takes on a new aspect if the people will be killed anyway and the property is the entire Earth.

Surprisingly enough, a familiar piece of equipment which could now reappear on future battlefields is the tank – dismissed as nearing obsolescence in Chapter 1, it could make a strong comeback if provided with its own miniature laser defences, thus becoming to a considerable extent immune to the missiles which are today driving tanks from the battlefront. Given this defence plus a back up in the form of heavy-duty composite armour, an improved tank could prove deadly indeed in areas remote from heavy-duty laser batteries. Perhaps there may be a future for those ogres of science fiction, the cybernetically controlled autonomous tanks (Keith Laumer's 'Bolo' machine or Andrew Stephenson's 'Voyo'; Colin Kapp in 'Gottlos' offers a version of these controlled by a plumbed-in human brain, but miniaturised computers are likely to become more robust and efficient). The great nuclear-powered machine would roll across the country, linked to reconnaissance satellites to warn it of activity over the horizon, radar and optical senses alert for attack, which with computer-swift reflexes it would parry with a sword of laser radiation; its missile-rack holds a selection of mini-nukes ranging up to city-buster size, while its big guns can fire guided HE missiles, nerve-gas canisters and half a dozen other useful things. It might require a saturation nuclear attack on one's own territory to eliminate such a marauding cybertank; either that or another machine of the same kind or larger. The infantry would be well advised to stay away.

And of course the computerisation can be extended to the running of the whole war. Every part of the force will now be tied together by radio and microwave links, backed up with low-power communications lasers; most of the messages rushing back and forth are likely to be in some form of machine-code in any case, and there is no great extrapolation involved in assuming that human speech will also be intelligible to the main computer network which is processing the battle-information. If sufficiently well programmed, the network (not a single computer but a series of linked ones across a country, with much redundancy to allow for damage to portions of the system) can make decisions very much faster than men – faster, indeed, than the relevant information could be conveyed to men. Certainly such a system will be needed to co-ordinate the satellite-information network, to act as watchdog on cybernetic tanks, to correlate radar and optical sightings of attacks on the home country; to feed advance information to the laser defences . . . adding overall control of the war to all this might be simple – or even a simplification. There would be misgivings; there would also be the disturbing possibility that the enemy had computerised his attack and that, without a full cybernetic defence control to oppose him, his reactions and co-ordination would give him a deadly advantage. Perhaps, indeed, a war might be fought more rationally and with less ultimate loss of life if the various contingency plans had to be thought out and programmed in advance, rather than being tinkered with by men under stress and working against time.

Considering that the next all-out war will very possibly be fought in hours, while even a 'slow-motion' war of resolution is unlikely to extend over more than a week, it seems only sensible to put a fast-thinking computer in charge. This would obviously not be a sort of servo-mechanism which pushed all the red buttons on the first attack, but a system possessed of judgements as well as speedy response. There is no difficulty in making a fast machine which can handle complex problems upon which men might labour for many lifetimes. An example is found in the proof of the four-colour theorem (which states that using only four different colours, any map drawn on a plane can be coloured so that no two adjacent territories share the same colour); this eluded mathematicians for many years. They developed exhaustive proofs that *five* colours would always be sufficient, and that *at least* four colours were necessary in the general case: but no one could show that four were both necessary and sufficient. Enter the computer, which when correctly programmed (a lengthy and complex task) began, in effect, to sort through *all* the possible basic forms that a map could take; in due course it announced the correctness of the four-colour theorem. Other machines – or, more correctly, other programmes – now play chess at close to master level; indeed, the pocket-sized chess computers play a pretty good game. From which it can be seen that, even if a machine cannot presently exercise true judgement, it can manage a fair imitation. It is neither daring nor original to predict that within decades the world's best chess player will be a machine;* so, before another century has passed, will be the world's finest strategist. Perhaps the intelligence of strategic computers could so far outstrip Man's as to lead them to the conclusion that the superweapons at their disposal are best left unused.

What superweapons? After all, one expects the future to be fearfully armed with devices which could if necessary wipe out all Earth life at a stroke. As it happens, the most likely means for achieving this undesirable end are merely extensions of things already discussed. In principle, a sufficiently large fusion explosion could knock the Earth out of its orbit (see Chapter 10). This is a rather pointless display of ostentation, since an explosion considerably

---

*Other games such as *Go* are presently less susceptible to machine analysis, a fact which sometimes provokes incredible displays of intellectual snobbery from *Go* players who like to denigrate chess as a child's game. When in due course a machine also becomes the top *Go* player, such people will no doubt move to games like snakes-and-ladders where computers have no detectable advantage.

smaller would send a killing shockwave through such parts of the atmosphere which were not blown clean away. In practice it's rather difficult to explode sufficiently large masses of lithium deuteride or whatever; the arrangement would have to be a fusion bomb which touched off further masses of 'fusible' material packed around it, which in turn set off still more: with the large masses involved, the superbomb would tend to blow itself apart without using most of its material. It should also be noted that few people are likely to wish to wipe out all life on Earth at a stroke, and a high percentage of these will be in straightjackets or otherwise prevented from building the superbomb. It is barely conceivable that some nation might construct such a device as a means of worldwide blackmail, either in the positive sense ('Fly ten trillion dollars in small used bills to the designated airfield or You Know What') or the negative ('Any attacks on *us* and you all die too'). One rather hopes not – such a strategy might easily provoke someone to call the bluff, which would be too bad if after all it was no bluff.

Slightly less dramatic but more feasible would be a more lingering version of the above death; a gigantic Dr Strangelove bomb to be exploded high in the air, a bomb built not so much for explosive power (the multimegaton yield is incidental) as for the tremendous amount of contamination it would release into those high airstreams which swept the dust of Krakatoa about the world. The 'great objectless bomb', it is called in *Deus Irae* (Philip K. Dick and Roger Zelazny). Perhaps many bombs of this sort would in fact be needed to emit the required fall out, an amount sufficient to kill virtually all of the world's people through radiation poisoning. No bang but a whimper: as the dosage builds up people are left vomiting and fainting, haemorrhaging from every orifice, hair falling out and skin sloughing off . . . the remaining choices being a suicide pill or the drab, recycled existence in the prison of a fall out shelter – while the food lasts. A fair approximation to this doom might be achieved by a sufficiently widespread shower of standard nuclear missiles, even if none would individually qualify as a final weapon.

Another weapon of great potential power – although not in the literally Earth-shattering class – is the gamma-ray laser, or 'graser'. We've already considered the X-ray laser briefly, and with no great optimism; a gamma-ray laser would be vastly more deadly – a true death ray – and vastly more difficult to make. The principle would be just as for normal lasers as discussed in Chapter 3, except that now we would not be concerned with the relatively puny *electronic* energy-levels but those of the nucleus itself. Protons and neutrons within the nucleus, like the electrons outside, appear to occupy rigidly-defined energy levels – transitions between these correspond not to light or X-ray photons but to the vastly greater energy of gamma-rays. Some gamma-rays are so lethally energetic that under certain circumstances their energy can be converted into the significant mass of an electron and a positron (anti-electron) – the process known as pair production. A gamma-ray laser would need a nuclear reactor to energise the nuclei – would probably *be* a nuclear reactor, like the UF_6 laser. The major stumbling-block is the necessary mirror: gamma-rays pass easily through light elements, while in heavier elements they dissipate their energy in pair production (which takes place only near a nucleus, the heavier the better) or *via* the Compton effect (where a gamma-ray photon 'bounces' off an electron and loses energy to it) or the photoelectric effect (in which *all* the photon energy is transferred to an electron which is then torn free from the parent atom). The mirror for a functioning graser would be no ordinary mirror; it represents a breakthrough in some field of physics which we cannot confidently predict – yet.

A final topic which deserves consideration is antimatter. As it happens, we have antimatter now, in the same way that we have access to the Philosopher's Stone. Gold (element 79) can be produced from mercury (element 80) by bombardment of the latter's nucleus, although only a few hundred atoms at a time – it would be cheaper to acquire gold by boiling a few cubic kilometres of sea to extract the kilograms of dissolved gold – and the tons of dissolved uranium, for that matter – from several thousands of millions of tons of water. Antimatter can likewise be produced in the laboratory, on a rather less lavish scale than synthetic gold, by a form of pair-production process. High-energy gamma-rays give electrons and anti-electrons, or, as it's written: $\gamma \rightarrow e^+ + e^-$. A similar nuclear reaction involving super-high-energy protons goes $p + p \rightarrow p + p + p + \bar{p}$, in which the energy of a very fast proton slammed against another is converted to a 'new' proton and an anti-proton $\bar{p}$ of opposite charge. If an anti-proton meets an anti-electron, they settle down together as a molecule of anti-hydrogen; two anti-protons and two anti-neutrons make a nucleus of anti-helium-4. (Both anti-neutrons and neutrons are uncharged, but they have opposite values of another important quantity called the baryon number, as do protons and anti-protons.) The antimatter elements are neither more nor less stable than the normal ones – anti-uranium will undergo a chain-reaction when a critical mass is primed with anti-neutrons – and they form compounds among themselves in the same way. But in practice anti-protons have a very short lifetime in our world, since they soon encounter normal protons and rush to mutual nnihilation – the mass/energy of particle and anti-particle being released in a shower of much lighter particles and gamma radiation.

In effect, when matter meets antimatter virtually the entire mass can be converted to energy – although to achieve the *total* mutual annihilation of a block of matter and another of antimatter would be extremely difficult, since the energy released would tend to blast the blocks apart upon their first contact. On the other hand, if a small missile of antimatter were hurled rapidly at a large body of normal matter the annihilation would be much more effective. We can calculate roughly the effects of a one-kiloton antimatter missile, using Einstein's relationship $E = mc^2$. Assuming that the annihilation is complete, with a total mass of two kilograms (one of matter and one of antimatter) being converted to energy, the resulting explosive yield is about $1 \cdot 8 \times 10^{17}$ joules, or a little under 45 megatons. A ton of antimatter combining with a ton of matter could yield an explosion of well over 40,000 megatons, which begins to look like a continent-wrecker.

Antimatter is far too expensive and awkward to be manufactured in the laboratory in any quantity, and likewise almost impossible to keep once made – since it will explode when touched by *any* normal matter whatever. Perhaps anti-iron might be suspended on and manipulated with magnetic fields: a whole range of science-fiction heroes have risked just this; for example, Jack Williamson's *Seetee Ship* ('Seetee' from CT or ContraTerrene, which is what early writers chose to call antimatter). The feat is reminiscent of the business called 'tickling the dragon's tail' in which masses of fissile material are brought close to demonstrate the increased radiation as the system approaches criticality; a mistake will not cause explosion for reasons detailed in Chapter 2, but *will* give a lethal burst of radiation. A piece of anti-iron suspended in vacuum (to prevent mutual-annihilation reactions with air) would have a far deadlier potential at some 43 megatons to the kilogram; if the magnetic fields should fail or become unstable, there will be a nuclear explosion. In any case, the anti-iron would continually emit high-energy radiation, since nothing can prevent odd molecules escaping from the walls of the vacuum container to strike the iron – and *vice versa*.

This deadly touchiness of antimatter may be a positive advantage should it be used as a mass weapon. There are no complications of critical mass, fusing or detonators: the question is simply one of bringing a suitable mass of antimatter into contact with normal matter. First find your antimatter . . . 'find' is likely to be the correct word, as even if some means of containing anti-protons were available (remembering that anti-hydrogen is normally a gas and must be frozen solid to be kept from the container walls) the time taken to amass a usable amount would run into centuries, while the cost would be astronomical. Anti-protons are manufactured at CERN and elsewhere for particle-physics studies where the collisions and reactions of relatively few particles are required; to make the 43-megaton antimatter bomb mentioned above we would need one kilogram of anti-hydrogen, representing about 6×10^{26} anti-protons (600,000,000,000,000,000,000,000,000).

But there is no reason why large lumps of antimatter should not exist in space; it could be that other parts of the Universe are composed of antimatter, and so occasional fragments of the stuff may drift our way. If a mass of antimatter should be found floating free in space, it would be relatively easy to handle – one need only squirt a little gas at it from a safe distance, and it will rush away, impelled by the energy-release of the matter/antimatter annihilation over part of its surface. Careful steering will aim it at Earth; precision timing by computers should make it possible to drop it into the sky of any nation. Precise aiming could be made difficult by its tendency to begin exploding as soon as it is within the atmosphere; but the great speed it will have attained should take the anti-meteor very rapidly, though pyrotechnically, to ground level. Precise aiming isn't all that necessary with a sufficient quantity of antimatter, since less than a ton should smash a medium-sized continent . . . It might be better to hope that there's no antimatter to be found within our Galaxy.

CHAPTER SEVEN

THE SOLAR SYSTEM

I: The Expanded Map

Up from Earth's Centre through the seventh Gate
I rose, and on the Throne of Saturn sate,
And many Knots unravel'd by the Road;
But not the Knot of Human Death and Fate.

OMAR KHAYYÁM

Holding on to the optimistic assumptions made much earlier, we can assume that, even if technological development is somewhat restricted by energy problems, it will still be possible to expand into space. Semi-permanent installations in close orbit about the Earth are no longer a novelty; the next steps should be to the Moon and to Gerard O'Neill's controversial space colonies. (Some prefer to say space cities or settlements, colonisation being a dirty word for more reasons than mere reference to the large intestine.) The military potential of the Moon was briefly discussed in Chapter 5; its basic tactical advantage over the Earth is that of a town built atop a high cliff, while Earth lies at the bottom. More precisely, Earth is at the bottom of a gravitational 'pit'; the Moon is in a much shallower pit at its edge, while the proposed L4 and L5 colonies would be on a sort of ridge between the main holes. The purpose of the catapult or mass driver in O'Neill's plan is to shunt building materials 'uphill' from the Moon to the colonies, thus making use of the iron and light metals which were found to make up 30% of the Apollo soil samples.

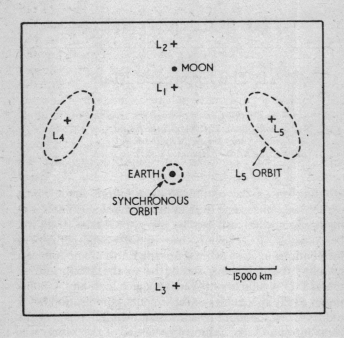

The L4 and L5 jargon which spills from prospective colonists' or settlers' lips refers to the Lagrangian or libration points of the Earth-Moon system as calculated by Lagrange himself in the 18th century. If the Earth and Moon were stationary relative to one another, there would be a balance point (L1) between them where their gravitational fields cancelled out; owing to their actual rotational movement, there are five balance points (fig. 5.). L1, L2 and L3 are unstable; objects placed there would be precariously balanced. But L4 and L5, the 'Trojan points', are gravitational traps which have already been observed to contain clouds of dust; owing to the influence of the Earth-Moon system's further motion about the Sun, the actual stable states involve describing curiously shaped orbits (dotted lines) about the points. These are in fact the only *true* stable orbits in the Earth-Moon system; tighter Earth orbits such as are used for satellites must eventually decay unless regular (although not necessarily frequent) velocity corrections are made. With a really large structure, like one of the proposed colonies, it is very difficult and expensive to make such corrections. Since L4 and L5 move with the Earth and Moon, the motion can also be considered as a distorted orbit about the Earth. The space colonies themselves would be immense structures holding thousands or millions of people, rotating to provide the illusion of gravity and powered by almost free solar energy. Solar energy is the bait which could lure men out there, since a solar cell in the best possible locations on Earth produces on average less than a tenth of the power which it would generate in space – where there is no rain, no cloud and no night. Moreover, there is no reason why a well made solar cell in space should not generate power for ever, requiring no cleaning or protection from the elements. Such power could then be beamed to Earth over the proposed microwave link, versions of which have already tested out at more than 55% efficiency as compared to a design goal of rather under 70%. (Actually most initial plans see the power satellites being established in geosynchronous orbit rather than at the more remote Lagrangian points: but O'Neill fans consider them merely the first step towards inevitable colonies.)

The prospect of this fearsome microwave beam being used as a death ray does not seem immediately likely, as various diffraction problems would make the target array (on Earth) perhaps fifty square kilometres in area, over which wide zone living tissue would merely experience an uncomfortable warmth. Admittedly the long-term hazards of low-intensity microwave radiation may be much more serious; and even in the short term the beam might be made incapacitating or lethal by increasing the power-input at the transmission end. The cost of all this, seemingly so much greater than that of building huge solar-cell arrays, is intended to be justified by much cheaper solar-cell manufacture and installation – continually upping the power return – by the supposedly now self-sustaining colonies.

Assuming the full O'Neill system of colonies at L4 and/or L5 supplied by a thriving base upon the Moon, how could war intrude into the cosy setup? The strategic positions are distinctly peculiar. Earth is handicapped by the colossal cliff of gravity which everything sent from its surface must climb – with the exception of beamed energy, unaffected by gravity (to a first approximation: Einstein's General Theory of Relativity shows how light climbing from a gravity well *does* lose energy – but in the case of Earth the loss is trivial). This is the great natural obstacle between Earth and the colonies, which are at the very 'top' of the gravity system; the Moon is also well situated by this criterion. Thus the layout of the battleground, with L4 and L5 each completing an equilateral triangle with the Earth and Moon as the other two points – as the Earth-Moon distance is some 380,000 kilometres, so also are the Earth-L4, Moon-L4, Earth-L5 and Moon-L5 distances, while L4 and L5 themselves are about 650,000 kilometres apart.

The weapons at the disposal of each of these centres are also varied. Earth has the full arsenal described at length already, but with much of it rendered less powerful or altogether impotent by the twin barriers of gravity and atmosphere. The atmosphere, conversely, provides considerable protection. The Moon has the catapult, a weapon which can take advantage of Earth's gravity well to damage it, and which could also quite effectively toss rocks towards the Lagrangian points. There is no significant atmosphere; surface-based power stations can drive lasers as potent defence weapons. Also, inhabitants of the Moon may well have dug deeply into the surface as an alternative to (or in addition to) the surface structures known to us all from science-fiction paintings. Finally, there is the L5 colony (or that at L4; they are equivalent), which is an exceedingly vulnerable structure possessing little but a huge solar power-source – the solar-cell banks which are the *raison d'être* of the colony. Obviously, if a future Earth is dependent on beamed solar power, the ability to cut it off is itself a powerful economic weapon; and, if a significant contribution is being made to the power-grid of the whole Earth, the tremendous amount of energy involved will give the L5 colony the option of mounting extremely potent laser weapons. Note that, although the range of a laser is theoretically infinite, we can probably discount their effective use over 380,000 kilometres owing to the problems of focussing alone. A nuclear-powered laser installation can cover a limited horizon with its laser fire; a solar-powered colony can observe and attack in every direction over a complete sphere; a shuttle from Earth will probably be at a severe disadvantage in terms of laser power, since it will lack the energy-resources of the larger installations. (As a *kamikaze* weapon, though, its mass would be sufficient to damage severely the delicate shell of a colony.) Note further that, although L5 may be the best strategic position in gravitational terms and thus the best place from which to throw rocks, the colony is not equipped to do so – there's no justification for building a mass driver in a place where there's nothing to be thrown. the one thing which could fall devastatingly to Earth is the colony itself – very much a last-ditch weapon! Earth is short on energy while L5 lacks raw materials; the Moon is able to run nuclear plants only if the materials are brought in from elsewhere, since hydrogen and heavy elements seem extremely scarce there. Solar power on the Moon is less cost-effective than in space, since the cells will be in darkness at least 50% of the time, and are less free to turn to an optimum position when the Sun *is* shining.

A final weapon in this interesting power-complex is both more subtle and more hypothetical – being the long-term effect of leaving the microwave power-links in operation. this is neither a war weapon nor likely to be recognised by the majority as one; but it is inarguable that *any* system which taps energy which would otherwise be lost in space, and funnels it down to Earth, may affect the climate. The proportion of the microwave beam which is reflected back into space would be negligible; that absorbed in the atmosphere (though absorbed much less enthusiastically than a light-beam of similar power) is directly converted to heat; that converted to electricity at Earth's surface will be transmitted along wires whose resistance changes some of it to heat. Ultimately, whether used for lighting, the driving of machinery, radio or straightforward heating, just about all the energy will end as heat. And we *do not know* how much excess heat can be added to Earth's weather system without causing a climatic catastrophe. This, of course, is a versatile argument which may be turned against any release of stored or unavailable energy (fission, fusion, coal-burning) as opposed to those energy-sources which tap 'free' energy (hydroelectricity, wind and wave power, geothermal heat).

Here, then, is a ready-made source of friction – even if they can be set up at next to no cost and turn an immense profit in energy terms, the space colonies are targets for the sort of criticism which has already been directed at the stored-energy power-sources. Even governments are responding to environmental lobbies, as witness the banning of fluorocarbon aerosol propellants in the US long before visible signs of the feared danger to the ozone layer, which helps keep off the more harmful UV rays. In addition to this, the solar energy would not be for everybody – only for those who could finance the gigantic solar-cell banks, the colonies (however small) which would maintain and expand them, and various 50-square-kilometre microwave arrays to receive the bounty from above. This could widen the rifts between haves and have-nots down below. Poorer nations are likely to be ill-represented in space in the future as in the past with the difference that so far it has been a restricted, dangerous activity (like mountaineering) while the colonies could easily be presented as controlled, pollution-free, Utopian environments with room for millions – although getting the millions there would be another matter and the selection procedures inevitable sources of friction. Unfortunately, the places so likely to cause contention are peculiarly vulnerable in the midst of vacuum: the vast windows required to admit sunlight might be a saboteur's dream – one medium-sized bomb to kill thousands on thousands of people! Of course, the terrorist who likes to plant a bomb and retreat to chortle over the carnage will be more likely to find himself literally in the same boat as the victims; besides, it would presumably take a huge explosion to evacuate a whole colony (with an air-volume of cubic kilometres) so rapidly that most people abroad could not don pressure-suits or rush to sealable quarters. L5 colonies will also be vulnerable to biological attack by infiltrators: with the whole intention being to run a system big enough to be virtually self-supporting through natural processes (food to sewage to crops to food . . .), a crop-killing virus or other pest could wreck the ecology without the old fear of a spread to the attacker's country, which is protected by 380,000 kilometres of emptiness. Terrorism can lead to larger and more serious incidents . . .

In the early days Earth would always be the ultimate arbiter, able to impose its will by sheer might. It could at any time kill the emergent colonies at L5 and upon the Moon by simple withdrawal of supplies; and, while not yet self-supporting, the men in space could only submit. Once viable, the colonies could withstand a simple 'starve them out' siege, although probably not any military intervention; in later days we can expect them to have sophisticated energy weapons at their disposal, quite possibly developed for initially peaceful purposes – particle-beam welding, long-range laser communications and even defence against meteors. (Remember that they are intended as *manufacturing* colonies with a prime product of new solar cells and bigger microwave power-beam transmitters.) It might be that with such defences, far more effective in space than in an atmosphere, the L5 and Moon installations would be able to withstand quite strong attacks. Such attacks might be launched as part of a conflict on Earth's surface, to destroy enemy power-sources, or by way of reprisal for some offence of the colonies themselves. For example, colonies deemed self-supporting but wishing more terrestrial aid in (for example) industrial development might try a little delicate blackmail, pointing out the ease with which the power-beams might be turned off, or diverted to point at cities, and large Moon-launched rocks flung down to Earth. The response would doubtless be a show of force.

Conversely, Earth governments might provoke defiance from above by demanding unrealistically high levels of effort – so many square kilometres of solar converter to be made operational in a given time, to meet Earth's needs, or else. The major exports of space will be intangibles – energy as already described, and knowledge gained in the unique experimental conditions of zero gravity with or without vacuum. In return, the L5 station would require raw materials which Earth cannot supply economically – they must come from the Moon. (this includes oxygen, which made up 40% of the Apollo 11 soil samples.) When an ecology becomes self-supporting, with long-established residents, there may in time arise the feeling that Earth has long since recouped its investments – that many instalments of that knowledge and power have paid off the mortgage on the hardware. Children are growing up on L5 who never signed their lives away for science. Yet inhabitants will still be expected to devote much of their time to running the solar-power conversion systems, mainly for the benefit of Earth. If history is any guide, this will eventually lead to a Declaration of Independence.

The analogy with US independence is interesting to consider. In the 18th century Britain was technically better equipped to wage war, but found itself unable to do so effectively with supply lines 5000 kilometres in length. Earth's military resources are still greater, but very few of them could be brought to bear against an enemy 380,000 kilometres distant and ringed with laser defences – especially since the 'estranging sea' is evacuated and vertical. Of course, an L5 colony would not be comparable in size with America (although the Moon is much larger); but the experience gained in such colonies could open up the whole of space for human habitation. And in a battle against space, Earth will always be fighting from the bottom of a hole.

II: Dogfight

Where ignorant armies clash by night . . .
MATTHEW ARNOLD, *Dover Beach*

By this time there will be enough traffic wandering around in space, commuting from Earth's surface into orbit (very expensive) and, more economically, especially if one is in no hurry, between Earth orbit, L4, L5 and the Moon. There already exist prototypes of the re-usable space shuttles from transport to and from Earth's surface; these, their boosters and the various satellite-launching rockets are the only forms of space transport which require streamlining. Vehicles travelling in space itself need none (unless they are travelling at relativistic velocities); typically they will look more like the Apollo lunar module – like a child's construction toy bristling with exposed girders and struts. This is not to say that all design principles can be abandoned in the playground of space – the craft will still need to withstand the acceleration of their own propulsors, and unless that push is carefully directed through the centre of mass of the entire system of craft and cargo there will be an unwelcome tendency to turn. This is not the 'artificial gravity' produced by spinning a vessel about its long axis like a rifled bullet; the turning moment resulting from an unbalanced thrust would shift the direction of the ship's long axis and thus of the jets themselves, causing the ship to describe wide curves like a sea-vessel with the rudder fixed askew.

But there is no rudder. The substances through which other vehicles move – aircraft through the air and ships through the water – reduce the efficiency of thrust because of friction, but also provide the means to generate that thrust as airscrews and propellors push against them. Without anything to push against, spaceships derive their thrust by throwing material away and effectively pushing against *that*. Sea and air vessels steer by allowing the medium's inevitable friction to act off-centre, producing unbalanced turning forces; a spaceship has nothing to slow it in such a controlled manner. Indeed it will travel for ever once it has acquired some speed, unless it hits something or is caught by some planet's gravity. A spaceship with one huge driver-jet can accelerate but cannot slow down or steer unless it is able to 'tack' about a planet, using the gravitational pull to change its course. A second, frontal jet could be added to decelerate the ship, but it's simpler to have one large propulsor complex and to turn the ship using small steering jets, thus pointing the main one in any desired direction. (Technically this could be achieved by shifting cargo about inside so as to shift the centre of mass. whereupon the off-centre thrust of the drive would rotate the ship; no one really takes this prospect seriously for a massive vessel.)

Manoeuvring in space will thus be a slow business. Having done a certain vast amount of work to reach a given velocity, one must do a similar amount to stop again, and it will take much the same time (unless for reasons of one's own one does not accelerate and decelerate with the same jet-power). The effort of making, say, a right-angled turn is still more daunting; simply to use the steering jets to turn the ship will leave one travelling the same way at the same velocity – sideways! One must, in fact, thrust backwards to kill the original velocity and also sideways to build up velocity in that direction. In practice the jet can be pointed at, say, 45° from straight-ahead to do both these things simultaneously, but still much work must be done to change course. On Earth we rely on friction – a skateboarder or cyclist can turn through 90° without much loss of speed by pitting his momentum against ground and letting the reaction forces change his course.

The inherent slowness of manoeuvring contrasts with the electronic speed with which it will be controlled. We can expect microcomputer supervision of the actual manoeuvring, with an inertial tracking system to follow the ship's actual accelerations and decelerations, plus (perhaps) some form of pattern-scanner watching the stars, which in space are always available to navigators (astrogators): all this can readily be mechanised. In time of war, our spaceship would in addition bear various weapons. These could include powerful lasers, space-adapted versions of the conventional light artillery, and small self-propelled missiles. Lasers have the huge advantage of delivery at the speed of light . . . but now we are working in space, they can be shielded against to some extent. Panels of ablating material, which could gravely endanger the stability of a re-entering missile, can be mounted upon true spaceships which make no concessions to planetary atmospheres. On the other hand, such added mass will decrease both the efficiency and manoeuvrability of a ship, since with more mass more fuel is needed for a given change in velocity; more fuel is required overall for a given trip; and still more is required owing to the greater mass of fuel which is being carried. Given this choice, a designer might opt for manoeuvrability – one cannot outrun or outmanoeuvre a laser but with forewarning from radar it could be possible to stay out of range (thousands of kilometres?). From the attacker's viewpoint the laser is a good weapon since it has *very* little effect on his ship's course – while artillery, for example, could administer significant 'kicks' from the recoil of each firing so that course adjustments would be required. Self-powered missiles also need have little or no effect on the launching ship; they will have the same choice between laser shielding and manoeuvrability as the large craft, but in a more acute form as in small objects a given thickness of shielding will form a greater proportion of total weight. Without the shield they can easily be damaged by the defenders' laser fire. In any case, ablative shielding is not perfect – it works by boiling away so that the laser heat is dissipated into space, and therefore prolonged fire *can* penetrate it (mirror-shields we've already discussed); moreover, the vaporised material is ejected with such force as to form a jet which can divert the missile's course; and of course shielded missile-guidance systems cannot guide by feedback from observation – if tucked away, protected from the outside world, they will have to operate inertially, taking the missile to a point where the ship attacked is expected to be. Depending on its manoeuvrability and the distance the missile must travel, the target ship may contrive to be elsewhere when the missile explodes – a few kilometres could be enough unless the attack er is using gigantic nuclear warheads.

A dogfight in space between evenly matched ships would be a strange, slow business. They would come into radar or optical view of one another, and instantly the on-board computers would begin to process the data: from radar echoes something can be told about the velocity of a body, as every motorist knows, although only about the component of velocity in the direction of the measuring system. That is, if the mystery ship were travelling directly towards the measurer, the radar would show its full velocity; if it were travelling nearly at right angles to that direction it would have only a small velocity component towards the measuring device. Movement in the perpendicular direction can be measured by noting the object's motion relative to the background stars. If the object is a hostile ship its computers will have been performing the same calculations. But how to tell a ship from a mere rock drifting randomly through space? Suspicions may be aroused if the object's path is not in the eliptic – that imaginary plane in which almost every object of the Solar System moves (notable exceptions being Pluto and the moons of Uranus) – or if the velocity and direction seem simply unlikely. If a rock is travelling so that x days ago its course must have intersected a planet's, this is suspicious. Likewise, without any such gross abnormality, an unlikely velocity can furnish a clue; any body orbiting the Sun must meet certain constraints of position and velocity, deviation being cause for curiosity. And, of course, if the object is under drive – perceptibly accelerating or decelerating and giving off a spume of excited molecules emitting radiation up and down the spectrum – the truth is obvious. the same applies when the object bounces radar beams off the observer ...

Friend or foe? Accidental meetings will be rare enough, for space is big – and one should know the locations of one's friends. Space, indeed, is so big that even in the narrow confines of our own Solar System a random encounter is not really likely ... but there *are* constraints on the paths to be taken, certain routes from Point A to Point B (not always the most obvious ones) which offer the best compromise between saving fuel and saving time. And radar will detect ships at a fair distance.

So the two ships identify each other as foes, and the battle may be on. The odds are high that their velocities will not match, that they cannot be made to match for hours or days, and thus that there will be time for no more than a brief exchange of compliments before each flashes again out of range of the other. In this case missiles and artillery will be of no avail unless the passage is improbably close: their use would be like fighting with bows and arrows between supersonic aircraft, with the target out of range before the arrow is fairly on its way. There remain the inevitable lasers, with which each ship can attempt at least to blind the sensors of the other. This is where machine fights machine, the fire-control computers racing to be the first to lock on to the enemy ship with a sighting laser, the reflected laser light exactly defining the target direction. Then the main lasers fire along exactly the same line. Since both ships are moving, the direction constantly alters and the beam is as constantly realigned; 'wobble' in the servo-motors which adjust the aim still prevents steady fire at the same spot. This has some advantages in that the shifting beam will play across the other's communication and detection gear, blinding the ship and giving the first to fire a decided advantage. Further attack may then melt a hole in the target's hull; the effect of this depends on the nature of the ship and the region damaged. One severed strut might cause negligible harm; or it could seriously reduce the ship's ability to survive its next acceleration/deceleration. Depressurisation of the main control-cabin is likely to be harmful; while in the (perhaps much larger) cargo area the only damage may be to cargo. Finally, even if the initial burst puts its target completely out of action, the attacker may never know it: his enemy will carry on seemingly unaffected.

With a little less velocity-difference between the antagonists, missiles can be used. Having an acceleration of hundreds of gravities (which would at once kill men) they can change velocity very quickly althugh not over long periods, owing to fuel limitations. Many medium-sized missiles can be carried today in a submarine; perhaps even on a spacecraft one or two could be fitted in. Such missiles can boost to many thousands of kilometres per hour in minutes; variants might track spacecraft for much longer periods, taking advantage of their low mass and high acceleration to catch the fleeing target and explode. A ship which loses in a laser-fire exchange may already have doomed its enemy by launching a nuclear missile which, some time later, arrives to avenge the dead . . . if it can contrive to avoid the inevitable laser defences.

The same applies to smaller missiles with micro-nuke or HE warheads. Semi-intelligent tracking missiles offer the best hopes: although a fixed-course missile might be aimed at where the extrapolated course of the target will take it (so that missile and target meet at that place) the travel time is likely to be great enough to allow evasive action. There was a similar situation in World War II, where anti-aircraft gunners had to learn to fire well ahead of the target aircraft; if they fired as instinct told them, the aircraft would no longer be there when the shells arrived; if they fired correctly, the weaving aircraft still might not go where expected. The time-lag problem applies with still more force to missiles like bullets and shells which are not self-propelled and cannot accelerate further.

This is the situation for what we may call call casual space combat – where ships just happen to run into one another (not literally) and fight. The general rule about brevity of fighting time owing to high relative velocity is likely to apply in other cases, as for example when an ambush takes place. Since a ship must have come from somewhere, and must likewise be going somewhere, a combination of espionage and suitably placed radar systems could give a prospective ambusher foreknowledge of his victim's course. There is very little in space that is unpredictable; no winds and tides are likely to turn the victim aside. The ambusher might build up velocity and allow his course to intersect that of the victim, their similar speeds now ensuring plenty of time for aggressive action as already outlined; or he might sow a 'minefield' in space, preferably at the last possible moment to preclude evasive action – this might be done by planting a nuclear weapon to shatter a suitable small asteroid, or on a smaller scale by a powered shrepnel-scattering missile which roams about on the predicted path of the victim until triggered. Even a single small rock would be likely to smite a moving ship with great force – if the ship is moving at a moderate 40,000 kph relative to Earth while the rock is not moving at all, their collision will involve the same energy that the rock would acquire by falling all the way to Earth: very considerable, as was shown in Chapter 5. In peacetime, no one would worry seriously about a dangerous meteoroid-impact (which has been shown to be very improbable) and thus would be unprepared for this trick; in war it would no doubt be a standard ruse, and ships would spend extra fuel upon seemingly random course-changes to avoid such carefully laid traps.

Not all encounters need be of the strangely static type. Space has no winds or tides, I said above: this is not quite true. There is the solar wind, a steady blast of particles and radiation from the Sun which does exert a tiny pressure – not enough to affect a standard spaceship, but enough to set the tails of comets streaming away from the wind. There are tides, not in space but in objects which move in space – any gravitational field causes tides, although in small bodies like spacecraft they are not noticeable (usually – see next chapter). And the actual shape of space is distorted near large masses; a gravitational field *is* a distortion of space. One can take advantage of this, as a racing-driver does of a banked track, to make course-changes. Approach a planet head-on and you will come to a sticky (or fiery) end; approach it more circumspectly, and at just the right speed, and your ship falls into orbit. By this we normally mean a closed and stable path; but there are orbits which do not loop back on themselves in tidy ellipses but open out into hyperbolae. A ship falling inward along one arm of the hyperbola has too much velocity to be trapped; it whips partly around the planet and off into space again. Without the tiniest thrust being exerted by the jets, the ship has made a major course change, allowing the planet to pull it into a fresh path. One can outdo this by well timed acceleration in the period of closest approach (perigee) – the gravitational PE of the fuel used, partly converted to KE in the fall, is not lost as the ship moves out again since the mass of that much fuel is no longer present; the planetary pull is less. The net result is that the ship now moves rather faster than if that fuel had been expended in open space.

There are tricks to be played in orbit on the same lines; in tighter orbits, closer to the planet, one moves faster (has to move faster). To catch someone ahead in the same orbit one does not fire the drive-jets, since that increases the speed, moving the ship tangentially out until the pull of gravity leaves it with lower KE but higher PE in a higher, slower orbit. But slight *deceleration* gives the opposite effect, dropping the ship into a tighter, faster orbit. This sort of gimmick has been handled at great length in SF, and none of these standard ploys should really have any surprise value: but who knows? Even a strategist may not think of everything; and besides, surprise is not always necessary when making use of strange ploys. A wrestler may know every throw in the book and be unable to counter them all; the fact that one *expects* the enemy to occupy the most advantageous spot makes it no less inconvenient when he does.

III: Further Out

He had bought a large map representing the sea,
Without the least vestige of land:
And the crew were much pleased when they found it
to be
A map they could all understand.
      LEWIS CARROLL, *The Hunting of the Snark*

Mars has for a long time been thought the next most likely living-place in the Solar System, after Earth: a place like a cold Earth desert with a thinner atmosphere. But, besides some possible small plants, it seems that Mars could better be described as like the cratered Moon with a bit more atmosphere. Venus too is uninhabitable – miles and miles of clouds above a surface which is unbearably hot and dark. It is conceivable (says Carl Sagan) that suitable algae could alter the atmosphere until Venus becomes Earthlike. This is a long-term plan; in the interim, the logical sites for distant colonies are the asteroids: little worlds with minimal gravity and, it seems, good supplies of metals. One could erect the traditional dome and dig into metal-rich areas: the excavation then becomes a larger, underground settlement. By occupying the volume rather than the surface of a worldlet, vast numbers of people could be accommodated . . . and the low gravity means that little work need be done to export the metals mined on slow trajectories (taking months or years) towards the Earth-Moon system and L4 or L5. Much of the production would be used locally: the asteroids could be a definite growth area. There is 'free' solar energy as usual, although rather less intense than is found closer to the Sun; for the same reason, the level of dangerous solar radiation is less, while the prospect of living underground in asteroids offers still more protection from such hazards. The extended scenario includes thriving industrial and mining colonies out in the asteroids, something similar on the Moon (but confined to the local light elements), the power-exporting colonies at the Lagrangian points, and perhaps a research station or two on Mars. Similar frictions to those suggested between Earth and L5 can be imagined between Earth and the asteroid mines, the main differences being (firstly) that L5 produces energy while the asteroids produce raw materials which are principally of use in space – since Earth has ample supplies of many raw materials but cannot afford to boost them into space *en masse*. (It may also be that rare and heavy metals needed by Earth will be located in the Belt.) Secondly, the lines of communication are now becoming stretched. The transit times between Earth and the asteroids are immense when one assumes rockets of the sort used today. For example, light takes something like eight minutes to reach the Earth from the Sun, four minutes more to reach the orbit of Mars and around forty minutes in all to the orbit of Jupiter: between Mars and Jupiter lie the thinly-scattered asteroids. The longest journey yet attempted by Man, to the Moon and back, can be made by light in less than three seconds. Can any governmental powers stretch across these awesome spaces? If an asteroid colony became self-sufficient, there would be little Earth could do along such tenuous lines of communication to prevent 'Belters' from doing pretty much as they liked. One small vessel *could* carry enough nuclear armament to smash an asteroid; but we can assume that a colonised asteroid would have all the standard defences already discussed. The Belt would also have some fearful potential weapons; a gigantic falling rock could be started on its long course to Earth from a secure base out there, and, if the riches of the rocks live up to the more optimistic expectations, there will also be the raw materials to manufacture nuclear armament on the scale of Earth's own.

Further out, to Jupiter and beyond, the skirmishes and even the simple requirements of existence become more and more difficult. The transit times move into years; acceptable for robot probes but not, perhaps, for men. Saturn is nearly twice as far out as Jupiter; Uranus more than twice as far as Saturn. All the expansion so far is a mere preliminary to the immense explorations to come . . . provided that we can find some way of taking the next long step into deep space.

CHAPTER EIGHT

THROUGH THE DARK COLD –

I: Slow Boat to Centauri

Miles, and miles, and miles of desolation!
Leagues on leagues on leagues without a change!
SWINBURNE, *By the North Sea*

Since the huge separating spaces of the Solar System alone are so vast and intimidating as to dwarf comprehension, and since our present technology offers little hope of penetrating in force to the great gas-giant planets (Jupiter and beyond) of this our own backyard, it may seem folly to look further out. But the outward surges of the last chapter involved large numbers of people, tons of cargo, a regular shuttle service – not needed in the first tentative probes. Already it's possible to take seriously the plans for L5 and lunar settlement; yet few men have reached the Moon and fewer have walked its surface. As the frontier moves outward, a few more will travel very much further – a questing rivulet which runs ahead of the main tide.

Our technology already offers the hope of much higher speeds than used in, for example, the Moon trips. In the simple black-and-white world of classical mechanics, one can accelerate to greater and greater velocities for as long as fuel is available. The fuel need not be the chemicals now used. A small nuclear reactor could flash water to high temperatures, boosting the ship upon a plume of steam which became a wake of tiny ice crystals . . . The water need not be heated – it will boil off into vacuum anyway – but, the hotter the steam is made, the faster it will leave and the greater the thrust. (Poul Anderson has even conceived a makeshift rocket driven by the incredible force of beer foaming off into space.) The fuel need not even be tangible; the 'ion drive' is simply an accelerator pushing single atoms or particles out of its muzzle: neutralised atoms for choice, lest the ship's accumulated charge cancels the thrust by pulling back the expelled particles. Even lasers can make jets – light has momentum, although a single photon has very little; each photon leaving the laser will impart an equal and opposite smidgeon of momentum to the ship. In the vicinity of a sun there's no real need for a laser; one merely spreads an immense aluminised-plastic mirror, a 'light-sail', and sails smoothly and with very small acceleration out from the sun. External lasers fired towards the sail will add to the thrust.

In the long term, it matters less that these more esoteric space-drives develop only a tiny thrust. A small thrust kept up for a long time is as effective as a great boost from a chemical rocket which will run out of mass to throw away at a fairly early stage of the journey. A laser needs no reaction mass, merely a sufficient supply of power, so that less energy need be used to transport fuel. If the power can be gleaned from space – from light near a sun, or from the fusion of interstellar hydrogen – the acceleration can theoretically continue for ever. One can accelerate for some time before becoming tangled in the effects of relativity . . . the velocities we've been considering so far begin with Earth's 40,000 kph escape velocity, which is around 27,000 times smaller than the velocity of light. The kinetic energy of a body increases as the *square* of its velocity: to travel 10 times faster we must generally do 100 times the work, since a 100-fold KE must be supplied. (With chemical rockets more work must be done in the early stages of the acceleration in order to push the fuel to be used in the later stages.) More energy must be kept in reserve to slow and stop the ship, and still more for the return journey.

A long-range vessel will perforce be able to release formidable amounts of energy: the drive can also be a weapon, especially if it's a multigigawatt bank of lasers. Even an apparently harmless 'steam-powered' ship using water for reaction mass could blind enemies with thousand-mile clouds of microscopic ice crystals, which might also soak up the energy of laser attack and form a partial screen. Drives of the more speculative type use a continuous nuclear explosion at the ship's rear (or a series of small pulsed ones, as in the British Interplanetary Society's 135 million kilometres per hour *Daedalus* starship design), emitting the shower of death which comes from a neutron-bomb fireball.

There are three main approaches to the problem of actually travelling vast distances with a relatively primitive technology, remaining well below *c*, the velocity of light. Sending robot probes is all very well, but men must follow in the end. One way is the 'lifeship', whose journey is limited very literally by the lifespans of its crew. Journeys to the outer planets – the first ones, at least – will probably knock years from the astronauts' lives. At a steady acceleration of one gravity (1g) a ship could reach 2,000,000 kph in under 16 hours, with the crew at ease since the acceleration would feel like normal gravity (the General Theory of Relativity insists that forces experienced from gravity and from acceleration are indistinguishable even in principle). At 2,000,000 kph we could reach Pluto in about four months, although to our neighbour star Alpha Centauri would take a trifle longer – over 2,200 years. And one would be more interested in travelling 6 light years to Barnard's Star, which seems to have planets, than 4·2 to Alpha Centauri, which does not. Unfortunately, even this modest speed is presently difficult to attain; a first visit to Pluto (not apparently a place so prepossessing as to demand our interest) may take years . . . and so we choose young crewmen.

The thought of spending years away from human society may be discouraging for prospective astronauts. A lifeship would certainly have to squeeze in more luxury than has been available in space: the authorities might have to try outlandish sanity-preserving tricks like mixing crews, which seem currently unthinkable. Any proper L5 colony will presumably include representatives of both halves of the human race, so the unthinkability of it all may be gradually eroded . . . thus opening the way for science fiction's standard First Attempt At The Stars: the 'generation ship'.

In a generation ship it is accepted that the human lifespan is too short for interstellar voyaging. Therefore the ship is a flying colony in its own right, upon which people live and die with each new generation being taught to handle the controls and keep the thing on course to its glorious goal. The commonest fate of fictional generation ships is forgetfulness of these tasks – disbelief of the young in the tales of old Earth, rejection of the notion that their 'world' is voyaging at all, and so on. (Alternatively they arrive to find that speedier ships built since they started have now colonised the stars.) If this can be avoided, such ships could scatter humanity across enormous distances at the cost of enormous time. It's a pretty safe bet that, no matter how successful the journey, if the ship does find another suitable world and set up a colony, there will presently be enough people there for a not-very-high-technology war.

Finally there is trickery with the lifespan. The bodies of the astronauts are frozen, to be revived when the long journeying is over. For this to work we need a means of freezing people without the formation of ice crystals, which rupture the cell walls and convert the delicate semipermeable membranes to a mess more permeable than a fishing-net. To overcome this problem the body must be frozen too fast for crystals to form. Even at absolute zero this is improbable; ice is a fair insulator, as in igloos and the lakes which so rarely freeze right to the bottom – once the body's outer layers are frozen the innards lose heat more slowly. Suggestions for overcoming this include saturation of the body with antifreeze and freezing at pressures so huge that water forms no expanding ice crystals. There is also a question of revival: the heart must be started, the lungs persuaded to breathe and the brain to think . . . and, since brief inactivity degrades a brain to something fit only for sale as offal, this last requirement is doubtful indeed. *Some* creatures have been successfully frozen and thawed, the most complex being fish. An advanced nervous system fails to survive. Fish make poor astronauts.

Better than freezing would be drugs which slow immensely a man's perception of time; some do exist, but none to make 100 years seem but a few, or which could be safely administered for 100 years in huge concentrations. (Cyanide makes a century seem like no time at all but, again, there is the revival problem.) Hypnotism and yoga may produce remarkable effects in the short term – the trance state with a heartbeat once in several seconds – but it's uncertain that the inexorable disintegration of body cells can be stayed by such means. Like drugs, mental disciplines alter one's *perception* of time without making much difference to the body's actual ageing. It would be traumatic to reach Alpha Centauri feeling the journey had taken scant seconds, only to find one's body a relatively young 150.

II: Starbow's End

But at my back I alwaies hear
Times winged Charriot hurrying near.
         MARVELL, *To his Coy Mistress*

One means of meddling with time is known. In relativistic mechanics, one's sense of time is slowed by living in a gravitational field or (what is the same) an accelerating vessel. Thus the General Theory: the Special Theory adds that time is seen to flow at different rates depending on the relative speed of observer and observed. The difference is subtle and quite difficult to check; shreds of proof for the theories have been found in the anomalous orbit of Mercury as it moves elliptically through the Sun's gravitational field, the bending of starlight past the Sun (seen only at eclipse – otherwise sunlight drowns the stars), the behaviour of that particle the muon (whose lifetime increases with rapid motion), and experiments in which atomic clocks were flown round the world at speed, after which their readings disagreed with stationary clocks.

Newton's classicical mechanics, which made the Solar System a great clock ticking off its celestial periods with only the slightest of annoying wobbles from Mercury, still holds today for everyday use; Einstein's mechanics is a corrected form of Newton's, only noticeably different when immense gravitational fields or very high velocities are involved. Relativity theory is startling in its simplicity: once the main assuption is accepted, the rest is simple algebra. The assumption of the Special Theory (proved experimentally) *is* staggering – it is that the speed of light is the same no matter what moving system it is measured from. A car may travel at 100 kph; to another car following at 60 kph its apparent speed will be only 40 kph: this is reasonable. But a light ray appears to move at just the same speed whether measured from either car or from a stationary point at the roadside. The algebra clicks remorselessly on from this point and announces that, to be consistent with the Assumption, the mass, length and rate of timeflow associated with any object will vary with its speed relative to the 'stationary' observer. The factor of difference is sometimes called τ(tau) and is equivalent to

$$\sqrt{1 - \frac{v^2}{c^2}}$$

if v, the velocity of the object, is much smaller than c then τ is nearly 1 and Newton's physics continues undisturbed. At 1,000,000 kph τ is very slightly decreased to about 0·9999991; to a stationary observer the length and timeflow of the moving body would shrink to this fraction of their 'normal' values, while the mass would increase by a factor of 1·τ to a staggering 1·00000086 of its stationary value. If the speed could be increased to 100 million kph, τ would rise to 0·9914; at 535 million kph, about half the speed of light, τ becomes 0·866. Time now flows at less than seven-eighths of its normal rate, while the ship's mass has risen by over 15%. We are becoming more and more speculative about the energy available to push the ship to such velocities; the assumption is that one day it will be available. *Unless* it is available, or more esoteric means of space-travel are perfected, genuine two-way travel between the stars will be impossible.

As c is more and more closely approached the ship's mass continues to increase and the timeflow aboard to slow. Such is the view which an outside observer would take; to those aboard, ship-time is quite normal and the reason they seem to cover distance so rapidly is that the distance between Earth and (say) Alpha Centauri appears shrunk by relativistic effects. At these speeds the Universe becomes increasingly strange to the traveller's eyes. Owing to the distortions of relativity the visible stars are crowded together ahead of the ship and more thinly scattered behind; thanks to the Doppler effect those ahead bluer and those behind redder than normal. (This meagre view of the 'starbow' has recently replaced the previous popular theory, whereby – as a result of our old calculations – it was expected that the stars would form wide bands coloured like a rainbow, surrounding a circle of near-total darkness directly ahead. It could be some obscure moral in the thought that this lovely and evocative image was the product of bad physics.).

Meanwhile, to the outside observer the mass increases so that the ship's resistance to motion is greater (mass *is* resistance to motion); each erg of energy from the drive contributes less to the velocity. c can never be attained, for then the mass would be infinite and infinite energy would be needed to reach that speed. Essentially, as c is approached, the drive-energy becomes extra mass and momentum – the velocity-increments become tinier and tinier. Here is a brief table of the effects:

Velocity (Fraction of c)	Shiptime Dilation (τ)	Mass Increase Factor ($1/\tau$)
0·1	0·995	1·005
0·5	0·866	1·155
0·9	0·436	2·294
0·99	0·141	7·089
0·999	0·045	22·366
0·9999	0·014	70·712
1·0	0·0	∞

So, at $0.9999c$ velocity, the 4·2 light-year trip to Alpha Centauri would take a little over 4·2 years to a watcher on Earth; to the ship's crew, which experiences time multiplied by τ, the trip would take under 22 days. That's if the whole trip were made at that speed; most of the time would be spent accelerating or decelerating, lengthening matters considerably. The real problem lies in the energy needed, a horrifying 1,000-plus megatons for each pound weight of the ship . . . This does make such relativistic ships into frightful weapons. The ship becomes an energy-accumulator, building up potential until it strikes with an impact energy of – well, if the ship weighs 100 tons, the energy release would be over 220 million megatons. Again it sounds like a continent-buster at the least! Such a weapon would be difficult to intercept since – at $0.9999c$ – it would be travelling hard on the heels of the light-rays of radar echoes which announced its coming. If it were aimed at Earth and detected by a Distant Early Warning system out near Pluto, the warning signal would take nearly 5 hours to reach Earth at the speed of light, followed by the doomsday machine itself about a fifth of a second later. This gives little time for defensive measures.

To achieve these velocities much fuel will be needed. The most efficient drive would combine matter with antimatter to obtain *total* conversion of mass to energy: even so, one must carry fuel. Still better could be the highly speculative Bussard ramjet. In theory, this spreads a wide net of magnetic fields before it, ionising the hydrogen atoms which infest interstellar space and funnelling them towards a fusion motor. Like a chemical-fuel ramjet (whose open end funnels in air for combustion) it will not function at low velocities; when moving fast enough it gathers the thinly scattered hydrogen at a rate sufficient to provide fusion fuel. Thereafter, the magnetic fields are maintained by surplus energy from fusion; no more stored fuel is needed. The faster the ship travels, the denser the fuel supply appears and the more efficiently the ramscoop can function. One can never reach c, but one can come arbitrarily close: $0.9999c$, $0.99999c$, $0.999999c$ . . . Outside, the processes of the Universe seem slowed and its geometry fantastically foreshortened. The clustered stars ahead crowd still closer together, brighter and increasingly blue-shifted; computers are needed to make sense of the galactic map.

And time is experienced at a very different rate. Although the ship already discussed may make it from Earth to Alpha Centauri in 22 days' subjective time, the trip will 'really' take over 4·2 years. A round trip *cannot* be completed in under 8·4 years. If travel between the stars can find no loopholes in relativity, then perhaps the time-lag will defuse explosive situations. Who would send a declaration of war, knowing that many years must elapse before it is even read? Couriers between the stars would slip ever further into the future, without hope of return, as planet-bound people lived out their lives and died. If the declaration of war were sent 100 light-years, then, although the courier might arrive in subjective days, the man who signed the paper would be long dead. Perhaps an implacable government might wage such long-term war across the centuries; more likely it would not survive that long. The wastes of time between star and star are criss-crossed with short cuts, but each is marked ONE WAY ONLY. The relativistic clocks may run at different rates: they cannot be put back.

To reiterate: according to Einstein any object having mass when at rest is unable to travel at the speed of light. Conversely, an object having *no* rest mass is unable to exist unless it does travel at c. Three known objects fall into this category: the neutrino and anti-neutrino, ghostly particles with no characteristics besides spin, and the ubiquitous photon. There is no such thing as a stationary photon – if one is stopped, it is transformed to energy in whatever material does the stopping. Radiation can be considered as showers of photons, the wavelength of radiation depending on the energy they possess. (Photons are schizophrenic, behaving like wave-motions or distinct 'objects' depending on the situation – let's keep that particular can of undulations firmly closed.) The need of photons to travel at velocity c does not mean that they must always move at 300,000 kilometres per second, the velocity of light in vacuum; in air light travels at only 0·99971 times this speed, while in water the speed falls to about three-quarters and in glass to about two-thirds of its value in space.

If our spaceship were converted to photons, it would zip through space at the velocity of light without need for tedious acceleration. We should have to provide some means of condensing it to matter at journey's end. The first difficulty arises from the sheer *amount* of energy corresponding to a given mass – equal to the explosive energy of nearly 10 megatons of TNT for every pound of mass. How does one arrange total conversion without resorting to destruction of the ship with an antiship, made of antimatter? Secondly, how is this fantastic burst of energy to be channelled and beamed to the required destination? We could as easily or more easily (the energies being less) channel an H-bomb explosion harmlessly into space or into central heating systems: an ultimate defence. However, these problems pale into insignificance compared to those of the receiving end, where some device must pick up the transmitted energy, less the inevitable losses, and squeeze it back into the original spaceship mass – preferably including the crew in as healthy a condition as before.

Such a transmission of mass/energy comes in two instalments – the raw energy and the coded signals describing how to assemble it into a spaceship complete with crew. Part of the difficulty can be eliminated by not sending the energy, just the assembly instructions – after all, the recipients will presumably have as much mass/energy to spare as the senders, and could very well use their own. The procedure is still not wholly convincing: it recalls a Leroy Kettle joke about publishing magazines by sending each subscriber a typewriter and detailed instructions on what words to type, and in what order. To reassemble a human body, those instructions must include not only the position of each atom of every molecule, but also the pattern in which they are linked and their directions of motion – the gross flow of blood and lymph, the fine atomic vibrations which determine temperature. It seems futile to convert energy to mass in addition: much cheaper to use existing mass. With a stockpile of 94 elements from hydrogen to plutonium, plus isotopes where needed (U-238 is no substitute for U-235 and vice-versa), the receiving station should have building bricks enough to assemble anything desired – if those vital instructions can be drawn up, safely transmitted (several times so that errors caused by noise between the stars can be eliminated) and somehow put into practice.

If *that* can be made to work, it would be amazingly easy to create a war fleet. One ship is built at HQ, the most expensive and well-equipped engine of destruction imaginable. It is crewed by the best men to be found. Then its structure – ship, weapons, crew, the lot – is scanned and beamed to where the ship is needed. Once the instructions have been received and recorded, the reassembly station manufactures ship after identical ship from the stockpiles of atoms to hand; the original need never be used. This interesting scheme will obviously be useful only when the cost of replication is less than that of manufacture by old-fashioned means; otherwise it would seem more logical to beam a conventional set of plans to the appropriate destination, where the ships could be built in the usual way. Considerably less technical advance might be necessary to send out a man – how about a cloned body at the far end, upon which the recorded and transmitted brain-pattern of the 'astronaut' might somehow be impressed?

In general, the least unworkable of these ways of sending things out at velocity *c* do not involve real travel but a replication of some original. The method is useless for shifting population off Earth. When applied to inanimate objects, replication is nothing new, really; when applied to people it raises theological problems (can souls be subdivided?) but may offer military advantages. Find your best man and multiply him into an army . . . if you can afford it.

III: Bending Space

Which is another name for that final scepticism which can find no floor to the universe.
G. K. CHESTERTON, *The Man Who Was Thursday*

Space is curved by the presence of mass; a gravitational field is a curvature of space. It isn't easy to imagine the meaning of 'curved' when the word is used of something empty and three-dimensional (what can it be curved through?); one analogy comes from a two-dimensional system. Draw a circle on flat paper and the circumference will be π times the diameter, π having its familiar value of 3·14159 . . . and the circle's area being π times the square of the radius. Now put the compass on a sphere and draw the circle on this curved surface: the circumference is *not* π times the diameter but something smaller. To put it differently, π is less when the surface is curved thus; the area of that surface enclosed by a 'circle' is less than for the circle of the same radius on a plane. π is not even constant on a sphere – if the 'circle' is small π approaches its normal value, while if it covers half the sphere's area π drops to 2. A sphere shows *positive curvature*; in such space π is smaller than expected and the area enclosed in a given radius is less. (Negative curvature occurs in, for example, a saddle-shaped surface – π is increased.) These effects have their parallel in 3D – a gravitational field produces positive curvature of space, and π is less near a mass so that a sphere of given radius encloses slightly less volume than expected.

Another anology involves a 2D model of 3D space, in the form of a flexible sheet (space) upon which various masses rest. A small mass produces a small dent in the sheet; a large one a distinct pit. This instantly offers a model of celestial mechanics, with the planets as lesser masses rolling round and round the Sun's deep bowl of gravity. A large enough mass might dent the sheet so deeply that even light could not crawl up the precipitous slope of gravity. When this occurs, the curvature of space in that region is so great that it has effectively closed itself off from the Universe. It has become a black hole.

A black hole is produced by a sufficient mass compressed into a sufficiently small radius. The conditions for a black hole are the same as for a body from which the escape velocity is equal to c, although the 'true' proof comes from General Relativity. A black hole is a highly strange object. All the distinguishing characteristics of the matter within are lost: it has radius, mass and spin, but nothing can be found out about happenings within the 'event horizon', the characteristic radius at which light rays aimed directly out never *quite* escape. From the viewpoint of the outside Universe they stand still for ever; all other light rays within the event horizon must curve back into the hole. (Actually this is true only for sufficiently large black holes. Small ones, with masses from ounces to many tons squashed into a tiny radius, tend to 'leak' – owing to the Heisenbergian uncertainty in the event horizon radius – losing energy at a vast rate until they vanish utterly.)

Normally a spaceship approaching a medium-sized black

MARS MASS   VENUS MASS   EARTH MASS

Fig. 6   Guide to black holes: these three blobs are the *actual sizes*
of black holes with planetary mass. A black hole of the Moon's
mass would be somewhat smaller than a full stop; with the masses
of Jupiter or the Sun the black holes are too large to show – about
5½ metres and 5½ kilometres across, respectively.

hole would be in for nothing but bad news. By the time the
hole is detected, it will probably be too late to save the ship
from being sucked down that fearful funnel of gravitation
to be annihilated at the central 'singularity' where curved
space comes to a point and the bottom drops out of the
Universe. Probably the crew would be dead before
reaching the event horizon, since the gravitational slope
would be so steep as to make tidal forces deadly; near a
hole of solar mass, the difference in gravitational field
between one's head and feet could produce a rending force
of many thousands of tons weight. As the Moon's field
humps up the seas on either side of the Earth, so the hole
would literally pull men in two before they ever reached it.

This is the grisly picture when the ship approaches an
ordinary black hole. For interesting results, it must seek a
hole of hundreds of thousands of times the Sun's mass –
then the event horizon is wider and the gravity does not
change so disastrously quickly. Destruction at the centre of
the hole still seems inevitable . . . unless the hole is *spinning*.
This is where the glib verbal explanations fail and scientists
flee shrieking to the consolations of mathematics: for now

it seems that one *can* escape the hole once more, and turn up somewhere completely different. The ship crosses the event horizon and circumnavigates the singularity at high speed, matching the spin of the hole itself. Without sinking to destruction at the singularity, the ship is somehow carried in a vortex of twisted space and emerges from the hole. It cannot emerge in our Universe, since that would demand that the velocity of light be exceeded. Therefore (to much muttering about 'the unacceptable face of relativity') it appears in another universe, instantaneously. It has dropped clean through that flexible sheet to land on another one 'below'.

So here is a way of using the strange paths of bent space to travel somewhere entirely other. It is hypothetical in the extreme. It opens up still more improbable possibilities like time travel – provided the ship can re-enter our original Universe. Probably return is *not* feasible, General Relativity hitting back by making it possible to attain endless universes – with their own scattered stars and black holes – passing through hole after spinning hole without any chance of return. (This overlooks the depressing possibility that if a black hole opens into another universe it is as a 'white hole' emitting the immense mass and energy drained from our Universe. For a ship it could be like emerging at the surface of a sun.) Optimists like Adrain Berry (in *The Iron Sun*) hope that a second hole found in the second universe will bring the ship back to this universe, only a long way from the starting-point – thus achieving faster-than-light travel without exceeding the speed of light. Only the most revolting pessimists would dwell on other calculations which suggest that the ship may be put through a sort of spatial mincer en route, to arrive in the form of highly disorganised gravity waves.

The problem is to find black holes of sufficient size and spin to be usable. Adrian Berry would rather like to build one close to the Solar System (we need only assemble a mass of many thousand times that of the entire system, squeeze it tightly together and let nature take its course); others prefer to hope that we may find a suitable hole ready-made, perhaps at the centre of our Galaxy. Perhaps.

Science fiction has always been ready to invoke new universes to facilitate space-travel. Usually one shifts into *hyperspace*, a speculative state of existence where speeds far greater than c may be attained. (Though there's a cruel George R. R. Martin story wherein after long research men burst into hyperspace and find that there the limiting velocity is *less* than c.) If the other space is not connected to ours in a simple fashion, a small movement *there* may be equivalent to one of many light years *here* – one flips into the different space, moves the ship a few yards and emerges again near a formerly distant star. Professor J. A. Wheeler has interpreted the equations of General Relativity to imply a superspace in which time does not exist so that all journeys will be instantaneous; and superspace is somehow linked to our own through innumerable 'wormholes'. Kingsley Amis notes that the limiting velocity c applies only to matter; there's no limit on how fast one can move *space* through space . . . so we somehow shift a volume of space at many times c, and in this volume our ship floats tranquilly.

'Doc' Smith's unforgettable (to put it gently) *Lensman* books offer a device which cancels a body's mass so that its speed is limited only by the resistance of interstellar dust. (Any force, no matter how small, would then send it off at c – it would bounce in a crazed Brownian motion from atom to atom of interstellar hydrogen, making manoeuvring difficult.) Harry Harrison has the 'Bloater Drive', which relies upon weakening intermolecular attractions so that the ship swells to many light years in length; the front reaches the destination while the rear is still at home – after which one allows the ship to shrink, keeping the front end fixed. There is the ship which bursts through the light barrier (emitting, of course, a photic boom) by means of extra-potent engines; there is the tube of force along which space itself is sucked by capillary action; and there is simple evasion of the issue by muttering of 'matter-antimatter pods' and 'warp factors' without worrying about the meaning of these useful terms.

No one expects a hard-working writer to outdo science in his understanding of space; yet one of these notions may well represent the simple verbalisation of a complex space-drive to be developed in the next few centuries. One blind spot we have not yet mentioned is the fact that Einstein's equations for altered mass, length and time do not forbid faster-than-light travel (FTL). They merely yield preposterous results *at* velocity c, where mass becomes infinite while length and time vanish. At greater velocities these quantities take on more plausible numerical values – but are now multiplied by i, the square root of -1. At velocity $1 \cdot 4142c$, mass, length and time are i times their stationary values. The interpretation of this remains dubious. it may simply mean that velocities above c are absurd (i is often called an imaginary number); it may mean that FTL travel moves our ship into another state of existence, its particles becoming *tachyons*, hypothetical entities which live 'on the other side of the light barrier' and are as incapable of falling to the speed of light as our tardier particles are of attaining it.

It is known that sometimes one does not have to pass through every point between A and B in order to reach one from the other. The phenomenon called quantum tunnelling permits an electron (or other particle) to shift across a region where it cannot exist, by the simple device of existing not in that region but first on one side and then magically on the other . . . as though someone unable to climb a hill could leak through to the other side. It's an effect of the Uncertainty Principle – an electron is spread through all space as a probability distribution, the probability being highest where we say the electron 'is'; favourable conditions (as in the tunnel diode) permit the electron to jump a small distance without existing anywhere between.

This might apply to the light-barrier problem. We can drive a ship arbitrarily close to *c*; and, although much better defined in position than a single electron owing to its greater mass, the ship does have some uncertainty in its position and velocity. If it could be *encouraged* somehow to exhibit a 'jump' very close to *c* – to change velocity infinitesimally and instantaneously to FTL without ever existing at velocity *c* . . . ? It's interesting to consider, but no more promising (one must come so *very* close to *c*, and the mass-increase reduces the jump possibility) than any other science-fiction notion.

Similarly placed is the logical extension of quantum-tunnelling itself. If an electron can travel instantaneously (well, at *c*) across a forbidden zone, why should a spacecraft not shift with equal ease across light years? The trouble is that, as we understand quantum tunnelling, even to shift a ship across the tiny distance covered in a tunnel-diode would require every electron and other particle of that ship to make that jump in the same direction at the same time. This might be like trying to boil a whole litre of water at the same time, so that it *all* shifts from water to steam in an instant. The random distributions of velocities would defeat one even if the heat-conduction problems did not. At present we can only speculate, and hope.

Finally there is the true space-distorter or matter-transmitter. Traditionally this is introduced by an analogy wherein all space is represented by a sheet of cloth; two points (stars) far apart on the cloth's surface can nonetheless be brought into contact by folding the cloth.

(This is not the same as the flexible sheet of the space-curvature model, one hopes; the thought of all those suns and planets rolling together as the cloth is folded is quite discouraging.) The points once brought into contact, one steps 'across' from one to the other. Translating the analogy into terms of 3D space, this means stepping in a direction perpendicular to either up-down or north-south or east-west: finding such a direction is generally left as an exercise for the reader. Another discouraging point concerns the shape of this cloth when several distortions exist at once; the thought of a permanent spatial knot, becoming more and more tangled as time goes on, is positively disturbing.

Skating over such difficulties, we hypothesise a matter-transmitter – teleportation device – which quietly and without fuss shifts mass from A to B. It may do so at the velocity of light, or instantaneously. In the former case, the Universe is as big as ever – jumps between stars take time, though presumably not subjective time, and the delays which defuse crises will remain. If the jump is instantaneous, the Universe at once becomes Earth's backyard if no apparatus is needed at the other end – otherwise expansion is limited by the speed of the slower-than-light ships which disseminate the apparatus. Low transmission-costs would mean a commuter's frontier – the raw, untamed planets would be no further from one's home than the local matter-transmitter. More likely, costs would be prohibitively high; a spaceship might always be needed since planets are liable to be moving at many lilometres per second relative to one another, and the traveller would have to match velocities with his destination before he could arrive. This all-too-probable state of affairs would provide enough separation in terms of distance and time to allow tensions to build up, while making travel sufficiently feasible to provide the means of war.

What kind of war might be fought over such a link would depend on the nature of the matter-transmitter itself. Larry Niven has compiled a handy directory in 'The Theory and Practice of Teleportation': the device might receive without requiring transmitting apparatus, enabling one to pillage the enemy mercilessly; it might be able to transmit without the need for receiving apparatus, in which case the first government to acquire the device can instantly teleport bombs to smash all its real and imagined enemies; or apparatus might be needed at both ends: in this case each side would have the power of veto over its own equipment, and could prevent the other from sending things by this convenient route – one imagines slower-than-light ramships racing to drop a receiver into the other side's vicinity, through which the true attack could be delivered . . .

The most horrifying possibilities perhaps stem from a hypothetical device which can bring two regions of space into effective proximity without being either. Poul Anderson's 'space-interference fusion inductor' linked its target's nuclei with horrifying results. On a larger scale, the victim finds space bending to bring his world close to a sun, or a black hole, or another world with high relative velocity which is hurtling on a collision course.

There again, he might by that stage be able to defend himself by shifting his planet to a safe and secret location, circling some distant sun . . . Perhaps like Lucian I should stop at this point 'for fear of exciting incredulity'.

CHAPTER NINE

FIRST CONTACT

I: A Voice Without a Face

The silent heavens have goings-on

WORDSWORTH

CETI – Contact with ExtraTerrestrial Intelligence – seems more likely to be first made *via* radio or laser than by physical encounter. Our signals to space began some time ago; Earth is now the most powerful radio source in the Solar System after the Sun, even though Jupiter emits considerable radiation. Signals of our presence have travelled tens of light years into space since the megawatt radar beams of World War II. We may have only to wait – one day someone will notice us, although perhaps not with special interest: 'Another piffling little civilisation – let them keep it up for 1000 years more and perhaps they'll be worth a closer look.'

It is a reasonable assumption that alien life exists out there. Most main-sequence stars have planets; most planets are likely to have the required elements for life; some of these will be in orbits neither too hot, tearing apart the evolving molecular chains, nor too cold, slowing chemical reactions to immobility (admittedly recent work shows that the 'habitable' zone about a sun could be narrow indeed); if life occurs and survives it is likely to acquire intelligence, which gives a species a strong advantage over all others, in the short term at least; intelligence as we define it leads to technology; of technological civilisations, a proportion will be neither undeveloped nor burnt-out . . . Estimates of the advanced civilisations in our Galaxy vary: there may be thousands. Some which have seen fit to advertise their presence will have died before the messages reach Earth; others may leave transmitting satellites which continue to Tell All to the watching stars after the death of local civilisation.

We may contribute 'Look at me!' signals to whatever inter-stellar communications there may be; a cheaper and perhaps a safer beginning is a little eavesdropping. Civilisations out there may be exchanging the secrets of the Universe; by all means let us listen. Admittedly such private conversations are likely to be directed along tight beams which Earth could not intercept, unless by some fortunate chance the beam passes through (or blankets) our own Solar System. More likely to be detected are undirectional signals – e.g., for local communication: a civilisation little more advanced than ours might emit *more* radio energy from the home planet than emitted by its sun – or messages actually intended for other races. If *they* are looking for *us*, the contact problem should be less.

But will it be? We know nothing of how aliens think. They might consider our Solar System incapable of supporting life ('That one's useless, Dwest – the third planet's thick with hydrogen oxide!'). We do not believe that any but carbon compounds are capable of the complexity of life; although chemistry should be the same everywhere, this view may prove parochial – and so may those of aliens. In any case, our undistinguished G-type sun is unlikely to compel interest. Even if someone has aimed his or her or its beam at our system, or is emitting so much undirectional power that no aim is necessary – for what do we listen? It's argued that a logical wavelength for interstellar communication is the 21-centimetre band, corresponding to the 'resonant frequency' of hydrogen, commonest element in the Universe (although oxygen is most abundant on Earth). The hydrogen line's frequency is of interest to all scientific civilisations – we think. *They* might think differently. It's also suggested that the logical, the only means of interstellar communication will be Q-rays: the ones we haven't discovered yet.

Known means of communication cover a wide enough range; there is the entire electromagnetic spectrum, from the lowest to the highest radio frequencies up through microwaves (radar) and infrared (heat) to the visible spectrum, ultraviolet, X-rays and gamma-rays, ending with super-high-energy 'cosmic rays'. Also possible are gravity waves (we can detect only fairly strong ones), neutrino beams (which we can barely detect at all – neutrinos pass with ease through the Earth, let alone detectors) and perhaps various forms of 'Q-ray': faster-than-light tachyon beams, for example. If we listen at the right frequency at the right time (they need not transmit full-time) with instruments pointing in the right direction (at one of many millions of stars), then perhaps a signal will come through. It will be recognised as meaningful through inherent irregularity – not the steady tick of a pulsar, with no more information content than a carrier wave, but something more patterned. We might have some difficulty with video signals not meant for ourselves, and plain alien-language broadcasts would almost certainly defy comprehension . . .

The simplest signal (if our aliens intend it for outsiders and think as we hope they will think) will be a train of pulses, many times repeated for the benefit of slow learners, which yields a binary number. Then, if all goes well, this number can be mapped on to a grid (binary numbers are all 0s and 1s: fill in a square for 1, leave it empty for 0 – or vice-versa, since tricksy aliens may have the opposite convention) to yield a picture (fig. 7). From this we should deduce reams of information expressed in terms which *They* find universally logical. They might not bother with such

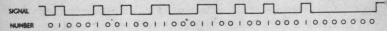

SIGNAL

NUMBER   0 1 0 0 0 1 0 0 1 0 0 1 1 0 0 0 1 1 0 0 1 0 0 1 0 0 1 0 0 0 1 0 0 0 0 0 0 0

PATTERN

Fig. 7   The signal given above yields the 35-digit binary number
01000100100110001100100100010000000 (or 101110 . . .: some
systems use the 'high' state for 0 and the 'low' for 1), which, when
mapped on to a 7 × 5 grid (35 has two factors only, 7 and 5, both of
which are prime numbers), sketches a carbon atom with its
massive nucleus and six electrons. This could tell aliens that
carbon is the basic element of Earth life, although other eyes
might see a planet with six moons or a gross obsecenity which
damns the sender utterly.

complications, preferring to provoke a response before
indulging in true communication. This would imply that
they sought contact with nearby races – otherwise the reply
lag might be immense. A signal with one pulse and a gap,
four and a gap, nine and a gap, sixteen . . . and so on,
repeating after a time, would assure listeners that this signal
wasn't natural and that its sender at least knew the squares
of the integers. The message is, in effect, 'Your move'. We
have a choice: to lie low and say nothing, or to step into the
limelight with a response.

Response is obviously expected, even when the communication is more than a 'Here I am' signal – perhaps
running into months of increasingly complex information,
each stage made understandable by those before. An
exception might involve a paranoid race which does *not*
want communication and which is prepared to eliminate
others whom it has never met and never wants to meet. For
example, the transmitted information could include details

of weapons so horrific – a means of detonating suns without effort, or of rupturing space to drop whole planets out of this mundane existence – as to virtually ensure the self-destruction of the race into whose hands it fell. Piers Anthony (in *Macroscope*) suggests a message deadly in itself – a sequence of inexorable logic which when followed to its conclusion destroys any intelligent mind. If this is discounted, and we are egotistic enough to assume that we can use wisely any dangerous knowledge which may come from space, then there's no harm in listening. But do we respond?

(In passing, note that in times to come humanity may just as well be responsible for the original transmissions in such an intended link; we would than be the 'alien' end of the dialogue, with the fear that some innocuous fact or equation of *ours* might have fearful effects upon aliens.)

The question of whether to announce our existence also arises when we have detected others talking among themselves, or who have betrayed their existence by (for example) building a Dyson sphere about ther sun to trap and utilise its radiation, so that only a leakage of infrared shows that civilisation has been at work. In such cases, when we know nothing about the aliens save that they command greater energies than ourselves (breaking up Jupiter and orbiting the fragments about the Sun as combined energy-collectors and living spaces is not yet within our capability), the choice is not easy. A vastly superior race might have no need or desire to eliminate primitives. As Philip Morrison has observed, if one sees a culture of bacteria forming themselves into letters spelling 'Don't disinfect our dish, we want to talk to you', one is unlikely to rush for the carbolic acid. Bear in mind that the emergence of more tedious primitives need not be of interest to a Master Race who have seen it all before – they might not bother to reply, either.

Assuming that we do respond, what do we say? Acknowledgement of messages received, yes; requests for clarification of parts not understood; information about ourselves, but not too much. Send too much on biology and They might tailor killer viruses to wipe us out; too much on psychology and they might understand and manipulate us better than we can ourselves;* too much on physics and they can deduce our military strength – or, worse, build weapons they had not thought of before owing to a different scientific philosophy. This again is the paranoid view; and even paranoids can be less so when the alien system is far away. Always there is the uncertainty: how *alien* are these aliens? If they tell us something of their history, something of the way they think, we may be reassured that we understand their logical processes: some assume that any race which develops high technology must of necessity think much like ourselves, but the assumption is doubtful. We cannot predict consistently the reactions of *Homo sapiens*, or of the animals who are closer to us than any extraterrestrial. Even when far-off contacts have minds which superficially run in the same 'reasonable' grooves as our own, we cannot know that the impulses below are even remotely conprehensible. Scientific logic may be a universal language, but it only conceals the tortuous emotions behind human attitudes.

There is another way for communications to take place across light years: here the advanced race, determined to contact others, sends hordes of robot ships which take up orbits about likely suns and beam messages at their planets (if there are no planets the sun is not a likely sun). If such a probe reached the Solar System we would have more to go on than beamed data. We could study the device itself and

---

*Poul Anderson has Earthmen destroying a repressive alien theocracy by beaming along cunningly devised heresies which split their Church. Certainly our history of casuistry and logical hair-splitting could make us well fitted for such warfare

with luck gain a fair impression of its makers' technical ability (then add years or centuries of development since the probe was launched). Such a probe might beam back a single message ('YES!') to its home on detecting local radio transmissions, plus astronomical data in any event. This would stop doubt and vacillation: they *know*, or will know in x years when the unstoppable message has made its way home, that Earth has a technological civilisation. How they are likely to react can be deduced only from doubtless inadequate information carried on the robot probe itself. Alien feelings are made plain if the device rushes Earthward and goes off in a multi-gigaton explosion. Meanwhile, if the velocity of light remains a limiting factor, we have $2x$ years before the aliens can even signal to us. (Otherwise they would more probably visit themselves rather than waste time on probes ... but again this assumes human motivations.)

We ourselves have made a small start in this direction, with pictorial message-plates aboard *Pioneer* exploratory probes which after studying our own outer planets went on into emptiness. Even the hastily prepared message first sent on Pioneers 10 and 11 contained more information than could be squeezed into a first-contact radio message ... although the perspective of the human figures shown may defy alien comprehension. The lady's genitalia are omitted out of concern for the feelings of human rather than extraterrestrial prudes.

Barring exotic means of offence – non-physical attack by transmission of damaging information – there is little to go wrong when communication is across a gap of light years of space, years of time. Like pen-friends in widely separated countries, the races can apply no sanctions in case of dissagreement, except cessation of contact. The contact is unlikely to be on a question-and-answer basis in any case: each side could send a continuous stream of information which it thinks the other should know. If one stops transmitting, x years of signals in transit will arrive before the other realises what has happened. With such frustrations to dialogue, one can imagine both races planning to meet once the necessary technology is developed. Perhaps then, like pen-friends who meet for the first time, they will discover surprising or unpleasant things about one another, which in the messages had been suppressed either innocently or by design.

II: Hands Across the Galaxy

Whoso sheddeth man's blood, by man shall his blood be shed.

Genesis ix: 6

The concept of actual, physical contact with alien intelligence is not precisely new. We already possess a vast literature upon the subject; it appears that alien contact has been practically incessant since prehistoric times. Admittedly the arguments supporting these theories lean on such assumptions as the total inability of our ancestors to haul rocks or perform simple calculations, necessitating the aid of omniscient and omnipotent alien helpers who repaid a little worship with a great deal of heavy haulage work and methematical tuition, while leaving virtually no trace of their providential presence. Even now, we are told, Earth's skies are patrolled by shoals of unfortunately no longer unidentified flying objects, whose only wish is to lead Man to salvation without being so unsporting as to reveal themselves to even halfway responsible people. (This curious approach shows how very alien the visitors must be.)

We now consider aliens yet to come, ones whose craft can be photographed without either fogging the film or bearing an uncanny resemblance to portions of old vacuum-cleaner. There are three basic forms which the first contact could take: we might journey to meet them, they might visit us in our own Solar System, or there might be a meeting on 'neutral ground'. There first two are essentially the same – race A travels to visit race B – but, since we are irretrievably identified with one race and would find it difficult to view matters with the strategist's impersonal eye, the situations have a very different emotional impact. Either could occur without warning to the visited race. The meeting on neutral ground, in some place alien to both parties, is less likely unless prearranged: two ships can wander for ever on the same sea, and still more so in space, without meeting. A port – a home solar system – will sooner or later receive many ships. We *can* imagine a chance meeting at some notable spot – at a spectacular binary star system like Beta Lyrae, or the hypothetical black holes of Cygnus X-1 or the galactic core – places which any race moved by curiosity might wish to visit.

A chance meeting in space might be no more than a brief sighting – the ionised wake of a fusion drive passing in the night, the relative velocities of human and alien vessels too great for contact to be made. Even with a mutual wish to meet, physics could bar the way – a relativistic ship might not have fuel for unscheduled decelerations and returns to near-c velocity in mid-journey. Even if it were able, too great a drop in velocity would add years to the crew's subjective trip-time – years in which food could run low and men die of old age. But if there is a meeting at some cosmic landmark, what then? Ideally both human and alien would be moved by scientific curiosity; both would roll up figurative sleeves and get to work on mutual communication. If instead the alien ship flees or launches an attack, we can conclude that They do not feel the same way. If they are friendly and communicative, this might be only a wish to probe our strengths and weaknesses, to find where we live so that they can smash these potential rivals. Such thoughts are inevitable. Whatever one's misgivings, aggression is also inadvisable until the warlike capabilities of the others are known.

The situation is pointed up in Murray Leinster's 'First Contact', where human and alien leaders regretfully concur that, reasonable though each may seem, neither dares to go home lest the other follow with nefarious intent. 'Neither ship could stake its own race's existence upon any conviction of the goodwill or the honour of the other.' Not wanting violence either, they hang about in an impasse until each contrives to blackmail the other to act 'reasonably' – i.e., trustingly. To be fair, it should be noted that a Soviet counterblast to this tale has man and alien meeting with no such capitalist forebodings: they greet one another with all the amity of interstellar Marxism, and depart in a haze of ionised vodka.

Communication is the essence of contact – which is why so many science-fiction tales have extraterrestrial wars caused by lack of understanding (this shows a touching faith in reason and goodwill). When actually faced with a strange vessel, the initial responses of human and alien need not be hostile. Suspicious, yes, and perhaps feigning friendliness in the base hope of acquiring strategically useful information – but when each side is wholly mysterious to the other, it would be unreasonable to open with overt hostility. (We hope that unreasonable beings will not make it into space.) So communication begins, implying an increasing exchange of information – which in the case of unexpected contact may be censored at short notice. Leinster's men even fudged up a star-chart in which stellar positions were *not* as seen from Earth – else its location would have been given away. Even language may have to be guarded in every sense – the English vocabulary contains numerous warlike words which could give the impression of a thoroughly nasty race – or of a technologically inadequate one, depending on the aliens. Perhaps one aim of synthetic alien-contact languages like Lincos is the avoidance of such embarrassments. Whole books could be written (and have been) concerning the reactions of hypothetical aliens to a present or future Earth culture. Time and again the slightest misinterpretation plunges all civilisation into war . . . again let's hope that our first aliens will be reasonable and tolerant beings. And that the humans of that day will be more reasonable and tolerant than now.

The business of information-suppression is of less concern when They turn up in our own system. The vital data of Earth's location are already theirs; unless they popped from some strange non-spatial transit system, we can also expect them to have spent an instructive time in their journey, studying all the radio and television broadcasts which we have so indiscriminately leaked out into space. In principle, visitors on arrival know virtually all about human society, bar classified information not generally transmitted about the place. True, they may gain as exaggerated impression of our racial love for music and six-guns, and likewise of our crime rate, and likewise of the importance of soap-powder and deodorants to earthly civilisation – but the essential facts will be there. Such knowledge can only enhance the smashing psychological impact of their arrival; it's a First Contact with humanity on the ignominious, passive side. (This is how it will seem when they find us; if we find them, humanity may feel one-up but the aliens need not feel one-down – their psychology is by definition alien.)

Again, what to do? First we must glean every scrap of

information about these visitors. Are they from an Earthlike planet, seeking fresh homes for their race? Have they terra-forming equipment – so that Earth could be adapted to their needs? This will be painfully obvious should the visitor be an alien generation-ship! Are they instead interested in one of the other planets? Gas-giant dwellers, for example, will never compete with us for living-space. Perhaps they have no colonial ambitions and simply wish to gather facts and establish peaceful contact. We in our turn must walk a narrow line between the perils of anthropomorphism and those of a Kahnesque game-theory approach to the situation.

The first danger is that of thinking them too much like ourselves, with all the human-like motivation which that implies. One can imagine aliens with whom we could *never* fully communicate, their minds being too different from our own. Fatal misunderstandings may arise if such creatures are ascribed a too-human viewpoint. It may be equally fatal to put our humanity aside and analyse the situation in cold-blooded terms of 'minimum risk, maximum gain'. This approach might dictate the attempted destruction of the alien probe – since its originators *could* have ultimately hostile intent, since there's only a small chance of its destruction being traceable to humanity, since the attack could easily be mounted using a 'friendly' shuttlecraft with a concealed nuclear weapon, since the ruined alien craft might yield valuable insight into a possibly superior technology and leave men better equipped to face future visits . . . Some passionless computer or politician might sum the factors and lead us into inexcusable folly. The consequences might be fatal, the aliens proving capable of resisting such attack and even of retaliatory measures. Even total success would scarcely be a matter for pride.

The ability to conceive such skullduggery could

admittedly be a strong survival trait. Since we are devious and cunning in our own right, it's easy to imagine men making *their* first contact in an alien system and casually announcing that a relay satellite has been established on the fringes of the system, ostensibly for innocuous reasons but in practice as an alarm-system to beam a warning back home in the event of dirty work. (If aliens visiting us *do* think as we do, they might also do this – not necessarily through real distrust but Just In Case.) It is certainly wrong to assume that *we* will always be benevolent and reasonable – the days of colonialism may be deplored in Britain and the US, but this didn't prevent the dispossession of Pacific islanders to clear the way for nuclear tests at Bikini and elsewhere. Should we meet a race technologically inferior to ourselves, even benevolence may ruin it – its people 'assisted' to become imitation Earthmen except for a few primitive tribes who spend their time inventing dances to amuse our anthropologists (xenologists). Perhaps something like this will happen here – weaned from our foolish terrestrial beliefs to the One True Way of Rigel's civilisation.

There is remarkably little to say about the possibility of encountering a *really* superior civilisation. We are restricted by our own view of civilisation . . . it's difficult to discard the feeling that anything superior is simply Earth society with knobs on, a bigger and better version of what we possess. As Brian Stableford says, we must liberate our hypotheses from the prison of our preconceptions. It may be that civilisations tend to reach a limit in their own system, huddling in Dyson spheres about a solitary sun; it may be that they leap from star to star at will. Perhaps there is a confederation of intelligences out there – the Galactic Congress, the Cosmic Circle, the Astral League! It may even be that in the hoariest of science-fiction clichés they are waiting for us to mature into possible probationary members; more probably, existing super-civilisations will be uninterested in a puny race like ours, which as yet cannot control the energy of even its own sun. If these mighty masters of space do exist, they would have no trouble in swatting out human life. The cockroach reaction: 'Ugh! there's life!', and *squelch*. Earth could be smashed, burnt, poisoned; the Sun detonated to erase all life in our system; the whole system, perhaps, isolated or sliced free of this Universe and cast into unimaginable regions beyond. Such forces appear in the next chapter – meanwhile, we should be very careful not to tangle with a super-race.

If there is no cosmic arbiter waiting to blow the whistle on offenders, it would seem that our greatest danger comes from races relatively near our own in development. The big ones are unassailable and probably uninterested; the smaller ones pose no challenge (and if we are sufficiently altruistic we shall refrain from interfering too much with *their* culture). Between are those like ourselves who will be exploring space from curiosity, hope of new living-space, and simple greed. There may be infinite *Lebensraum* in space, but the vast majority of it will be unavailable to us intermediate races. Assuming that (say) one solar system in 100 has an Earthlike planet which we could settle or adapt for settlement, each fresh world we find will represent 100 (on average) trips to unknown systems. With such an amount of research tied up in each world discovered, their value will be out of proportion to their true abundance; moreover, we are limited to systems within range of Earth itself (or later, within range of an established colony).

This world-oriented viewpoint assumes that it will someday be economic to shift populations through interstellar space (or to transport valuable power-metals; unusable worlds might just be strip-mined). In practice, without a cheap matter-transmitter colonisation is merely a way of establishing human outposts in defiance of what C.

S. Lewis called 'God's quarantine regulations'; the colony worlds may acquire vast populations as nature takes its course, without effect upon the crowded Earth. Earth's present state is already reminiscent of that legendary line of marching Chinese which never ceases; millions of people could be lifted into space each day without even keeping pace with the birthrate. Population control at home could reduce rivalry over worlds; perhaps then there will be little cause for conflict with alien races – barring competition for materials like power-metals, and the misunderstandings and accidents which can always lead to war. Even so, the expanse of pursuing war across interstellar space will be very great, especially without cheap FTL travel. If you can travel conveniently between the stars, you can field terror-weapons which can probably erase life from whole planets, as was hinted in the last chapter, by deploying the fearful energy of a relativistic ship or by setting up deadly non-spatial links between the enemy planet and somewhere inhospitable like the core of a sun. The balance of terror which holds our present-day arsenals in check may be still more evident in a galactic society of the future.

CHAPTER TEN

MACHINERY
OF ARMAGEDDON

I: Measuring the Unthinkable

I've measured it from side to side;
'Tis three feet long, and two feet wide.
WORDSWORTH, *The Thorn*

So far the most appalling destruction we have properly
considered has been conveniently measurable in terms of
the explosive force of TNT, one megaton approximating
an energy release of 10^{15} colories ($4 \cdot 2 \times 10^{15}$ joules). More
energy than this is released each second by human
civilisation: our total power consumption approaches
10^{16} wattes (joules per second). On a suggested scale for
measuring the energy controlled by super-civilisations, a
Type 1 civilisation is one having power on this scale
available – for communication or destruction. Earth
doesn't quite make it as a Type I civilisation, as much of
our power use is tied up and cannot be diverted into the
torrent of raw power which we might theoretically
produce. This refers to continuous power-output; for
example, some 20,000 megatons-worth of nuclear
weapons might be exploded in the worst versions of World
War III now conceivable, and if they were all detonated
in a single second the average power-output over that
time would be close on 10^{20} watts. But we couldn't keep
this up.

The next major step up on the scale of technologies is the
Type II civilisation, one able to deploy a power-output

equivalent to that of a typical star . . . around 10^{26} watts. Our own Sun releases some four times this power, continuously. Such a civilisation, if it used its available energy destructively, could manage a continuous destructive output of one million times the intensity of the 'unthinkable' nuclear spasm used as an example above – the equivalent of 20,000 million one-megaton bombs falling in each successive second, for as long as necessary. If such an attack were directed against a single planet, it's hard to think that the necessary time *would* be very long. In this example and in others to follow, the *how* remains obscure; if the writer knew how to acquire and manipulate these gigantic energies, he might by now have won the Nobel Prize and/or conquered the world.

Our own technological expansion could take us to Type II status if unchecked. The expansion from Type I to Type II capability means an increase in available power by a factor of 10^{10}; at an annual growth rate of only 5% this could be achieved in 472 years, or 242 years at 10%, or 126 years at 20%. Such a pyramiding of compound interest demands that the growth rate be maintained – civilisation must not crash through war or poverty – and that no limits are encountered. Similar calculations show that bacteria in a culture-dish can multiply until after a short time they outmass the Earth. In practice, they reach the edges of their culture medium and then run out of food. If Earth is our only culture-dish, we will soon be near the edge; but in the Solar System there is energy enough to take us to Type II level, freely dispensed by our Sun.

The Solar System only becomes a confining culture-dish when we consider the step to Type III technology, able to control the energetic output of an entire galaxy – say 10^{36} watts, 10^{10} times the power available to a Type II civilisation. Colonisation of a scattering of planetary systems does not necessarily raise mankind towards Type

III level – at best the 'conventional' means of interstellar travel will lead to a number of isolated Type II colonies, each utilising something close to the total output of the local sun, each cut off from most of the others by gulfs of space. We can provide estimates of the cost of liberating energy on the Type III scale within a solar system. Assuming total conversionn of mass to energy, a type III civilisation could consume its 10^{36} watts for under 200 years before using up the entire mass of the solar system, excluding the sun; counting in the sun as well, the time is extended to approaching 140,000 years – still not reassuring if the civilisation plans to endure. It may be that energy can be pulled from unpredictable sources – that universes of energy now undetectable may be trapped and drained – in which case a relatively young culture might at any time make a break-through and be boosted to Type III. There is a suspicion that much of the mass of the Universe is locked in black holes; when these are combined into larger black holes, much of their mass can be extracted as energy – though *how* remains uncertain. This is perhaps a last-ditch power source, a means of lingering on as the stars expire as the only lights in the Universe are artificial . . . or old light weary from long travel, bringing the images of galaxies already dead. Let's return to the warlike ability of a relatively puny Type II civilisation.

The traditional space-operatic super-civilisation is wont to smash planets which cause it offence – not, that is, subdue or subjugate them, but break them into little bits. To disperse a planet completely needs an energy on the order of its own gravitational energy – which is a measure of the strength with which it holds together. An explosion which could utterly wreck the Earth in this fashion would be of about 10^{16} megatons – say 10,000 million million one-megaton hydrogen bombs detonated simultaneously. Though this would mean diverting the power resources of a

Type II culture for only about 0·1 nanoseconds, it does somehow seem wasteful. The aggressor has no need to pulverise Earth so completely; if he were content to blast the outer mile or so of Earth's crust off into space, only a thousandth of the energy would be required; and this amount could be halved if the seas were spared and his fury directed only against the land. This still leaves several hundred megatons of destruction for each man, woman and child of Earth's present population. Spectacular but not economical.

Indeed, fewer than 200 million one-megaton bombs would be needed to provide one for each square mile of Earth's surface. We are coming again to the delivery problem. It may be easier in war to squander ludicrous amounts of raw energy than to indulge in the precision work of 'economical' destruction. A one-pound weight dropped from a little height will kill a man; multiply the energy required by the population of the world and it turns out that the energy of a one-megaton explosion, if properly deployed in falling one-pound weights, is enough to slaughter everyone on Earth several hundred times over. Economics can be taken to the point of absurdity. It may be that the human race will always be too much trouble to wipe out . . .

But the traditional super-villains have other options at their disposal. They might, for example, simply stop Earth in its tracks (an unfortunate metaphor where planets are concerned . . . c.f. Tennyson's 'Let the great world spin forever down the ringing grooves of change'). The orbital KE of the Earth is around 6×10^{17} megatons, so that oddly it's many times easier in terms of pure energy to smash the planet completely than to stop it moving round the Sun at its accustomed 30 kilometres per second. If stopped relative to the Sun, Earth will have no velocity component to carry it aside as it inevitably falls; it will be consumed in a gigantic fusion reaction, although life will have been extinguished through sheer heat long before the planet reaches the solar photosphere. This does offer a cheaper means of making oneself unpleasant on Earth: a shift in orbit should be adequate to snuff out life. To shift Earth 20% further from the Sun would mean an energy increase of 10^{17} megatons, causing a 31% reduction in solar heating of the Earth and thus an aggravated Ice Age. A 20% inward movement requires that Earth's overall energy be *reduced* by some $1\cdot6 \times 10^{17}$ megatons; in this closer orbit solar heating rises 56% and presently the oceans boil. It should be noted that any large-scale tampering with Earth's orbital motion is not only far more costly than destroying the planet but also needs more precision. Presumably a world can be destroyed in a single more or less soul-satisfying explosion, while with the sheer energy required to shift or halt it the planet seems likely to get broken in the process. Short of either attaching huge reaction-drives to the world, or smiting it with a comparable mass, the thing is not really credible from our present viewpoint.

One moderately cheap thing which could be done is to halt the Earth's rotation. Considerably less energy is involved – the rotational energy is only about 6×10^{13} megatons. On the other hand, the operation is still more delicate than the orbit-shifting already discussed; one must use either (a) a frictional-braking approach, using unbalanced reaction drives, or interference of Earth's magnetic field with an external one, or possibly gravitational braking by tides such as the Moon's, which are very gradually slowing Earth's rotation; or (b) a brutal and uncouth method involving direct coalescence of the Earth with another body having opposite rotational momentum. Immanuel Velikovsky suggests that if another body with opposite spin *is* to hand, angular momentum can be cancelled *via* immense electrical discharges, thus causing the Sun to stand still upon Gibeon. No one has been able to try the experiment, loose planets being hard to find; but to stop the Earth would undoubtedly set the crustal plates jolting together in earthquakes huge enough to melt portions of Earth's surface, throw up fresh mountain ranges and generally cause alarm. (Velikovsky does allow that such effects toppled the walls of Jericho.)

If one really wishes to erase a planet, the gross mechanical means can be expensive. Should the planet be sufficiently advanced to be worth wiping out – one, that is, which can offer opposition – then its inhabitants can presumably see careering asteroids as they approach and take some form of action: shattering the oncoming mass into fragments or diverting it from its course. This could be made difficult by using a black hole as the weapon; one of Earth's mass would be less than two centimetres across, making it close to undetectable except by its gravitational effects on the Solar System as it passes through). Nuclear explosions could not destroy it; nothing destroys a black hole of this size or larger. Indeed, the proportion of a nuclear fireball which affected the target presented – less than three square centimetres – would be negligible. Earth's only chance would be to throw enough fast-moving matter into the hole (which would pull objects in to the same extent as Earth itself) to alter its motion before it drew near enough to perturb Earth's orbit seriously. If it came close it could become a binary planet-system with Earth, which would produce merely cataclysmic effects of giant tides, earthquakes, etc.; if well aimed it would intersect the Earth itself and swallow it. The hole would fall towards Earth's centre, and as it fell Earth's substance would fly into the hole and vanish from space as we know it. The end result would be a slightly larger black hole, having twice

Earth's previous mass. There would be a final burst of intolerable brilliance as the last shreds of Earth were squeezed together down that funnel of gravity; then nothing but the little moving blot in space, still less than two centimetres across, drifting on with the impetus of all Earth's momentum and spin in addition to that with which it started. Probably it would fall into its own orbit about the Sun: a monument.

How does one move so deadly as object as a black hole? One must either feed it with fast-moving rocks whose transferred momentum make it go in the desired direction; or with electrical charge so that it may be accelerated electrostatically from a safe distance. There is no limit to the charge which can be put on a black hole; anything else must reach a saturation point, but the hole retains everything.

This weapon, and others of greater or lesser power (antimatter, falling asteroids, relativistic missiles), can smash a planet. If Earth goes, the Moon will either be destroyed or will fall into a fresh orbit: L4 and L5 stations likewise. This leaves a possible human colony on Mars, another on a potentially terra-formed Venus; scattered settlements upon various asteroids and the moons of Jupiter or even Saturn; outposts, perhaps, still further out from the Sun . . . By the time a planet-smashing war becomes even moderately likely, the human 'enemy' is dispersed over billions on billions of miles of space. Ditto for advanced alien cultures. Is it possible to fire a shot heard all around the Solar System, something which will sterilise most or all of these targets without excessive trouble?

Such a weapon may be available to Type II civilisations. The astrophysicist Geoffrey Burbidge has speculated that high gamma-ray fluxes can cause stars to erupt into supernovae. Carl Sagan suggests that gamma-ray lasers might achieve this effect over interstellar distances; such a laser could be beamed over 10 light years or more with so small a beam spread as to produce a 'spot' only a few miles across on the surface of the target sun. By Burbidge's estimates, the beam would require an input power of only about 3×10^{15} watts – less than one megaton per second – to trigger the supernova reaction in a normal main-sequence star. (The period for which the irradiation must be kept up is uncertain.) A supernova would almost certainly sterilise our Solar System; and the cost, even assuming that years of attack are required, is moderate from the viewpoint of a Type II technology. The result is a gigantic flare of radiation – lethal at distances of light years or more, and which Burbidge surmises may detonate nearby suns – plus huge ejections of mass as heavier elements are thrown out in sufficient quantities to form new planetary systems. Here is a motive for causing 'peaceful' supernovae: vital mass, the basic raw material of all technology, is released – mass which otherwise would remain locked in the core of a sun until it cooled or went nova or supernova through natural causes. Perhaps in the future a gamma-ray laser will be aimed at our Sun by a mass-starved Type II technology; it may be that they will realise too late that Earth is inhabited by radio- and TV-using beings. The aliens will have their regrets – one hopes – but by then the gamma-rays will be on their way in a long beam stretching across light years, unstoppable.

Maybe in a few centuries we shall take the same gamble ourselves, perhaps taking care to choose a sun without planets, perhaps not. Ethics can be forgotten when a race believes strong measures are necessary for its survival ... or maybe only its convenience. Even when care is taken, there remains the chance that the planetless 'bachelor' sun at which the beam is directed will detonate and in its turn trigger more suns in a chain reaction; in denser regions of the galaxy such constellations of supernovae might grow beyond control. There may be stabilising factors — absorption of radiation in dust-clouds, or the presence of a large black hole. Still, it's been suggested that our own galactic core could already have run away in this fashion — in which case we should know nothing of it for perhaps thousands of years, until the wave of lethal radiation arrived. Conceivably an attack on this colossal scale might be used to sterilise whole galaxies, although not exactly 'at a stroke'. However, we presume that only a culture outside a given galaxy would genuinely wish to destroy it (although accidents can happen within). The millions of light years which separate our galaxy from others should be protection enough against extragalactic attack in the absence of FTL transport — the attack would require an aggressor who took offence at signals millions of years old, and wished to take a fearful revenge on the descendants of those responsible, millions of years further in the future. A more plausible attacker might be a Type III galactic civilisation which wanted to lay up a store of mass for the future.

With FTL travel, we might expect a galaxy to become unified to an extent — *via* exchanges of information at the least. It all depends on the form of FTL travel: if it's an instantaneous matter-transmitter, a culture's influence may be limited by the speed (less than *c*) with which it can disseminate its receiving apparatus. Without the need for receivers — in and out of spatial wormholes — the limit is still economic. Even if one can travel at will to any of a million stars, one can't visit them all at once without a million expensive ships or a million expensive matter-transmitters . . . Therefore selection creeps in: one travels either to systems where likely planets and resources are hoped for or to those containing already contacted intelligence. There may be several cultural networks (reflecting the tendency of races to seek ones like themselves) which may join at systems containing planets of more than one life-supporting type (as ours has Earth, plus marginal life-supporters – for us – Venus and Mars, plus potential homes of very different life on Jupiter and Saturn). With physical contact between intelligencies that are already known, the picture is of expanding 'spheres of influence', since initial non-physical contact is more probable when contacter and contactee are relatively close. Ultimately, with true instantaneous travel, everywhere is next door to everywhere else and there is no reason why the network should not spread ultimately from galaxy to galaxy.

In the early days of such 'unlimited' expansion, there may never come a motive for war. If travel is cheap and easy, if planets for colonisation are plentiful or races few, the economic motives said to start most wars may never come into play. There remain political motives – an obvious example being that of a military government justifying its continual martial law by maintaining conflict with someone outside. Or religious motives: and those who consider the things which have been done (and are still being done) on Earth, in the name of religions preaching brotherhood and goodwill, can have a fine pessimistic time listing the possible intolerances of alien theocrats.

But, in the end, economics will squeeze the most amicable of galactic cultures with its bony fingers. While the stars still burn, energy will be there for the taking; but that part of the mass of our Universe which is not locked in stars or black holes will become precious. Planets will be broken up to increase the available surface area for living, huddled about the suns in Dyson spheres to intercept as high as possible a percentage of the available radiation. Environment need no longer be of any concern – the Type II civilisations can engineer any chunk of rock into living-space. The suns provide all needed energy; the fight is for mass. Some cultures will curb the ancient urge to increase their numbers, and achieve stability; some will wish to continue unchecked, and cast covetous eyes upon the suns and the hoarded mass of those more restrained. By this time, suns without natural planets will either have been colonised with belts of artificial planets, or detonated and their raw mass scavenged. A 'stable' galaxy comes when one expanding civilisation, or a finite number of stable ones, is all that survives. the expanding one can then struggle with itself or learn at last not to expand . . . Such a situation may endure for many billions of years while, one by one, the stars go out.

Free energy *must* run out. The suns spend their fires; only by suns are the various fuel materials produced (uranium in the cores of old stars, coal and oil indirectly by conversion of solar energy in plants). Interstellar hydrogen may be used to stoke the suns awhile, but eventually it will be profitless to send ships scavenging for such tiny returns. The remaining civilisations may fight over the Universe's scattered mass, or be forced into co-operation. The last phase may be the longest in the life of the Universe, with stars that shone a mere memory; intelligent life may linger for aeons by judicious use of the stored energy in black holes. Nothing can be extracted from a single black hole; but by combining two, up to 29% of the total mass can be released as energy. If the total mass is about that of the Sun, the energy emitted is on the order of the total radiation emissions of perhaps a dozen stars over their complete lifetimes. Using the convenient units of megatons of TNT, this is over 10^{31} megatons; sufficient energy to shatter 10^{15} planets of Earth's size, or sterilise a far greater number through heat and radiation, or – converted to power with only 10% efficiency – power a Type II technology for a million million years and more. Unless titanic matter-antimatter explosions can be arranged, the collisions of black holes produce the largest single bursts of energy possible in the Universe as we know it. Except, of course, for the primal Big Bang which started the whole intricate drama of mass and energy which has been playing ever more slowly in the millennia since.

II: Considering the 'Impossible'

We are between the wild thoat of certainty and the mad zitidar of fact – we can escape neither.
EDGAR RICE BURROUGHS, *The Gods of Mars*

If we allow an escalating technology sufficient time to expand, it will generally be able to perform the impossible – that is, feats impossible to us. Miracles will take a good deal (or even infinitely) longer, where a miracle is defined as something impossible under today's reading of the laws of physics. It is the difference between being unable to lift a weight (although knowing that a stronger man could do so) and being unable to snap one's fingers and transform the weight into a feather (which violates the law of conservation of mass/energy, to say the least). The trick of prediction is to decide which ultimately fall into which category. Some put their trust in physics as it stands, and class anything impossible at first glance as impossible always; others accept that present theory may yet suffer radical new interpretations, or may even fail to apply in other places and times.

Each age is limited by its own conception of the Universe. As the Victorians saw a totally predictable, clockwork Universe with a future of bigger and better steam-engines, so our own prophets suggest starflight through huge devices powered mechanically by advanced jet-drives. A true optimist may hope for something less predictable without knowing just *what*. The laws of physics as seen by theorists are already in a constant state of flux, and almost anything may emerge when the paradoxes are resolved. Speculations in this book have relied heavily on classical mechanics, the laws of thermodynamics and relativity theory – plus the great 'unchallengable' assumption of science sometimes called the rule of mediocrity; this says roughly that in other parts of space (and thus of time, for each photon of starlight is a message from the past) the *fundamental* laws will be the same as they are here and now.

We can, for example, assume that the rules were the same in Newton's day. The vast compendium of data from which he deduced his Law of Gravitation is consistent with today's knowledge of the Universe; more accurate measurements would have revealed tiny relativistic corrections, but it's perhpas as well that Newton did not have to make two great leaps of understanding rather than just one. Newtonian mechanics was *correct*, for Newton's time; it agreed with all available data and thus by William of Occam's principle of parsimony it was correct – then. The principle, called Occam's razor since it cuts away inessentials, insists that the 'true' theory is always the simplest that accounts for known facts. Although useful and even commonsensical in practice, this can be unpopular with rigorous logicians to whom even space and time may be unwarranted assumptions. It can be argued that the principle produces over-simplistic theories; so it does but, *if* the truth is more complex, the simple theory still remains adequate until more accurate data contradicts it – whereupon Occam's rule demands an improved theory! Newtonian mechanics is good enough even now for many purposes: the relativistic corrections are subtle and often insignificant. Einstein's mechanics *seems* adequate today;

we can find no inconsistencies in its view of the Universe. One day further corrections may be required. Then omniscient observers might note that the inhabitants of Sol III have discovered a further infinitesimal fragment of the Truth; from *our* viewpoint it might as well be said that the laws of physics have changed.

We can see science in a state of flux in today's chaotic particle physics, where sometimes in the welter of tantalising half-solutions it seems that the simplest answer may be that God exists and is a confirmed practical joker. But when Napoleon asked the mathematician Laplace whether he believed in God he was told 'I have no need for that hypothesis'; the principle of parsimony has so far ensured that the same applies to physics. Some think reality is best sliced with Occam's razor into page upon page of neatly tabulated data; some insist that it be swallowed whole as a single mystical bolus. The latter may offer beauty and mystery, but the former gets results.

Occam's dividing line marks off the knowable from the unknowable. On the 'knowable' side we have the panoply of today's theories of physics; beyond are theories of things presently unknowable because presently incapable of proof or disproof. A celebrated example is the hypothesis that somewhere in the asteroid belt is an object a foot across composed entirely of chocolate cake. We cannot disprove this without visiting the asteroid belt and spending many years looking . . . and even then believers in the hypothesis might merely insist we had not looked carefully enough. (Many pseudoscientific theories are inherently impossible to prove or disprove, like Bertrand Russell's spoof suggestion that the world was created five minutes ago, complete with false history and memories.) Similarly, the principle of mediocrity can only be disproved by finding a region of space/time where laws are different – or circumstances under which they take on new meaning.

For example, it's easy to suggest that the laws of thermodynamics could be reinterpreted. The first law, the law of conservation of massenergy, states that energy cannot be created or destroyed; the second, that entropy always increases – that is, that disorder increases and the available energy is always less as its distribution becomes more uniform. (Add ice to hot water; you cannot split the resulting lukewarm water into hot water and ice without doing work on it and expending more energy.) Asimov paraphrases the first two laws as 'You can't win' and 'You can't break even either'. The third concerns the unattainability of absolute zero, at which temperature energy transfers *could* be made without losses – the paraphrase might be 'You can't even stay out of the game'. *No exceptions to these laws have been found*. Ultimately they foretell the heat-death of the Universe, where energy is scattered in unusable form – stagnant and dead. But assume that the first law applies only overall, to a number of universes. If we can make a hole into another universe, its energy can be tapped and brought here in a constant stream. The law is not *broken*, since another universe is losing energy; but from our viewpoint the first law no longer applies. If the number of universes is infinite (and why not?) we can tap the more energetic ones for power, while unusable waste heat can be discharged into cold, empty universes. Such loopholes could make the laws of thermodynamics no problem. Similarly, Chapter 8 has suggested ways of slipping around or through the constraints on travel. Almost anything may be possible, however unlikely it seems in our own small perspective. Or all these things may be 'miracles' which cannot be performed by any technology capable of being developed in our Universe before it finally runs down. We cannot say.

There are other feats which we can presume will *never* be possible. Travel through time, for example, offers the unparalelled warlike opportunity of going back to overcome your opponent before he is aware of your very existence! This leads to the most vicious paradoxes (if you destroy your enemy in this retrospective fashion, he no longer exists and therefore you have no need to return in time to destroy him – and therefore he was never destroyed, and does after all exist . . .). The production of paradoxes in some more eccentric black-hole speculations has even been used in reverse as an argument against General Relativity; but we only assume that a paradox is an 'unthinkable' state. Laws of the Universe we have not yet encountered may provide in some way for their resolution. However, Larry Niven offers a neat argument against changing the past: since the use of time machines throws the 'real' past and future into a state of turmoil and flux, the only stable universe is in fact one where time machines are not invented and never will be. All other universes keep changing as a result of tampering until they chance to reach the stable state. Or the past may be unalterable in any case – one can go there, but impotently. Or an alteration to the past may merely create a new universe in which the alteration took place, which is no help to us in the original unchanged universe. Time travel either doesn't work or cancels itself out.

Another science-fiction dream, immortality, is quite reasonable – if the immortality need not extend beyond the lifetime of the Universe. 'Computerised' immortality as suggested in Chapter 6 does not seem very far away; 'real' immortality would appear to require that entropy be held back in the body, which is too complex a system for repair. The solution would be cloned bodies, with old brain-images being transferred somehow to new hosts . . . Classical problems which seem much simpler, like squaring the circle, have been proved utterly impossible for all time. Perpetual motion in the ideal sense is forbidden by the first law of thermodynamics: virtually perpetual motion can thus be produced if the law can be interpreted as above, and energy stolen from fresh universes. Perhaps if the inhabitants of those places complain we shall have an ultimate inter-universal war.

Manipulation of gravity is not obviously impossible. It is not, however, likely to be achieved by anything like H. G. Wells's Cavorite, which insulated objects from gravitational influence. Gravity is a curvature of space, a twist in the structure of the Universe – nothing can stand in its way since everything material must conform to the shape of space. We can oppose gravity – pieces of furniture, for example, are static engines for doing just that – but we can no more cancel its influence with a magic insulator than stop a landslide by drawing lines on the ground before it. Theoretically, there are two ways of overcoming gravity: one can either oppose it with an applied force (chairs push one up, a rocket engine pushes harder) or cancel it by *altering* the shape of space. This could be done by holding another planet the size of the Earth immediately above Earth's surface – using very stout props! The opposing curvatures would cancel – space, relative to the Earth, would be locally flattened – and there would be no gravity save that of the Sun, Moon, etc., in a narrow zone between the two Earths. This is not a convenient form of 'anti-gravity'. The notion of cutting off from a planet's numbing gravitational pull and flitting unchecked about the cosmos appears less and less likely. If one *could* drift up into the sky there would be inexplicable changes in potential energy, unaccounted for by any system of book-keeping; for, if gravity has no influence on a ship powered by the X-drive, no energy is needed to shift it from Earth's surface to infinity – and the energy that *should* be used could accelerate the ship to 40,000 kph. The ship can turn off its X-drive and fall back to Earth, acquiring all this energy

(*Alexis Gilliland,* from *Science Fiction Review*)

from nowhere. Rocks can be floated into the air and dropped – perpetual motion.

This same argument does, of course, apply to matter-transmitters. We can only say that either energy is coming from or going to another universe, or that it comes and goes from the ship itself. Niven suggests, for example, that potential-energy differences between matter-transmitter and receiver manifest themselves as temperature changes – jump over too great a difference and you are boiled alive or frozen solid. Or the X-drive may just not be possible. The *point* of anti-gravity in this form is that it is a reactionless drive – a genuine space drive. A true reactionless drive violates Newton's third law (action and reaction are equal and opposite) – but again there may be ways of faking it. If the drive pushes against something 'outside' our space it will seem reactionless in this Universe, although not in the supernal overview of (for example) Olaf Stapledon's Star Maker, who sees all universes simultaneously. Note that in this case energy is lost to the universe pushed against . . . All this, however, may be nonesense. We are in the position of dreamers long ago, who could imagine men flying but had no inkling of the future technologies required to perform this miracle.

If the X-drive is possible, there is no limit to its application. Instantly we are in the grandiose space-operatic world of E. E. Smith, where whole planets fly into battle only to be countered by missiles of planetary or greater size; or the more logical future of James Blish's *Cities in Flight* books, where planets *could* be made to collide but no one is so wasteful as to do it. Every such act, natural or artificial, in war or peace, is after all another increase of entropy – another step towards the very end, when all the mass of our Universe has puréed itself through black holes and singularities into an endlessly uniform distribution of energy, and time itself ceases to have a meaning. Nothing can prevent the steady progession towards this end, but careful hoarding of mass and energy could delay it for countless billions of years. On the planetary, stellar or galactic scale the message is the same. War is a luxury Man cannot afford . . . but Man has a long history of putting luxuries before necessities.

AFTERWORD:
Logic of Expansion

If we could near them with the flight unflown,
We should but find them worlds as sad as this,
Or suns all self-consuming like our own
Enringed by planet worlds as much amiss:
They wax and wane through fusion and confusion;
The spheres eternal are a grand illusion,
The empyrean is a void abyss.

JAMES THOMSON, *The City of Dreadful*
Night

It could easily be thought that warfare is the inexorable
result of Darwinian selection; that, as in the ruthless
struggle for survival beast contends against beast and
insect against insect, so warfare is the means by which the
men best fitted to survive (be they purest Aryan, WASP or
strugglers for black power) will inevitably crush the puny
ones who stand against them. Natural selection – naturally
– does not work in quite this way; it is a subtle matter
extending over countless generations, where the genes
giving one subspecies an 'edge' will gradually lead it to
predominance. the doctrine is 'survival of the fittest', but it
does not follow that in every case the fittest must survive;
the random dice-throws of mutation may more than once
have produced a super-beast which was better fitted to
survive than any of its kin, and which yet had the hard luck
to be stepped on by an iguanadon on its last legs before
extinction. The iguanadon's massive clumsiness made it
less fit to survive, not more, than our ill-fated mutant;
likewise the fact that one 'subspecies' of humanity has more
nuclear weapons than another does not make it necessarily

superior; nor do Darwin's holy words justify it in attacking all others.

The genuine process of evolution through natural selection has left Man with a brain superior to that of any animal. Superior in his own terms, that is, just as a cockroach would be King of Beasts if it were making the rules. It's even been argued that Man's overdeveloped brain is as much an evolutionary freak as the fantastic mass and armour of the dinosaurs in their final decadence – and as much of a handicap. More so, perhaps, for the dinosaurs survived for considerably longer than Man's recorded history to date, while his hypertrophied intelligence is capable of destroying him in the next century or so. It has, for example, led him to invent interesting pastime of organised warfare. Margaret Mead noted that war is no more a natural instinct than others such as 'writing, marriage, cooking our food instead of eating it raw, trial by jury or burial of the dead . . .'. There are tribes who have not this invention, who never fight wars; such people might be better fitted for long-term survival than those whose prowess with clubs, swords, guns and bombs has made them into mighty nations.

On the other hand, a paranoid outlook might lead us to argue that, although to be simple and live at one with nature could be fine for a species in isolation, it is of no use when bloodthirsty aliens come to dispossess us . . . Besides, the best way for a species is not necessarily best for the individual. The life of a simple peace-loving tribesman is generally nasty, brutish and short. And only technology offers any hope of surviving the inevitable death of the Sun, or of extending the life of our race to something near that of the Universe itself. Intellect is a survival mechanism in the very long term – or would be were it not plagued with demons.

Natural selection certainly does work against the

YOU NEED PROOF WAR IS
IRRATIONAL? THE GERMAN
GENERAL STAFF LOST
MORE WORLD WARS THAN
ANY MAJOR POWER...
AND EVERYBODY ADOPTED
THE GEN-
ERAL
STAFF
CONCEPT
FROM
US!

(Alexis Gilliland)

disinterested intellect. The brain which survives is the one whose deepest instincts say *Survive!* and the species which survives is programmed with the directive *Reproduce!* In Man's early days this was a most cogent instruction and one embodied in tribal law; yet intellect could override instinct, as when the unfortunate Onan became the first recorded user of *coitus interruptus* and was duly reproved. The need to maintain tribal numbers is enshrined in many religions, has been propped up with much theological justification and now persists in times when the intellect has industriously done away with much of the disease and attrition which made necessary the force of that command *Reproduce!* (Not that Earth shows signs of becoming an Utopia the potential may exist but so, obviously, do inequality and greed.) The human race follows its antique drum and continues to expand.

And continues, and continues . . .

The distressing exponentials which govern the theoretical multiplication of bacteria apply equally to multiplying humanity. At the present growth rate, for example, the mass of humanity will exceed the mass of the Earth itself in less than 1600 years. Perhaps contraceptives will prove the greatest benefit science has yet produced . . . but one cannot help remembering Cyril Kornbluth's black little story 'The Marching Morons', in which over many years the people with the intelligence to realise the necessity duly take their pills; others do not; and the result is that the numbers grow as before while the average intelligence of mankind takes a nose dive.

Perhaps Robert Heinlein had a point after all, when he recently suggested that a good rousing World War III would be a fine thing for the human race. It would at least reduce the numbers. Better to have it sooner than later, or course, for there is no telling when a *real* doomsday weapon will emerge – better to suffer a nuclear holocaust now than total annihilation in a few years or a few centuries . . .

Again this is the logic of the very short term. Long-term survival depends on a continuing high technology (windmills cannot replace nuclear power stations unless there is a terrific population crash to reduce demand); in the really long term it seems to depend on a foothold in space. War has brought us a long way, has driven us into producing a technology capable of what, in terms of only 100 or 50 years ago, are miracles; at some stage, though, it really should be abandoned. The machinery of war gave Man his first chance at space – for that it must be thanked – but we should not let sentimental regard for the toys of Cradle Earth seduce us into the greater and greater holocausts possible to an escalating technology.

The future will doubtless remind us time and again that, as J. B. S. Haldane put it, the Universe is queerer than we can imagine. The real future of our race need not be reasonable: there may yet be a super-technology which gives us individually the powers of gods, a super-philosophy which is incontrovertibly the One True Way and outmodes all previous fumblings for the truth. It may be that – following the children of Clarke's *Childhood's End* – humanity will gladly renounce its humanity in favour of something greater, even before the lights of our Universe fade and technology is settled for the long siege of the dark. Presumably war will be with us for the forseeable future; but finer things may lie ahead, and if we refrain from suicide our descendants will have the chance of finding out just what these are.

ACKNOWLEDGEMENTS

Although any errors in this book are mine alone, the following people and organisations deserve thanks for their assistance in various ways. Special thanks are due to Christopher Priest and my wife Hazel, for reasons they well know.

Dr C. W. D. Andrews; Avco Everett Research Laboratory Inc; Jim Barker; Paul Barnett; Tony Berry; Ben Bova; the British Interplanetary Society; Bill Dillon; Dermot Dobson; Malcolm Edwards; Hilary Evans; Mrs M. C. Evans; John Foyster; Richard E. Geis; Alexis Gilliland; the Hale Observatories; Robert Holdstock; Alan Hunter; Dr S. K. Hutchinson; the Imperial War Museum; Rob Jackson; Jon Langford; Mac Malsenn; Angus McKie; M. H. McTaggart; the Ministry of Defence; Peter Roberts; Michael Scott Rohan; the Royal Astronomical Society; Short Bros & Harland Ltd; Ken Shutler; Andrew Stephenson; G. S. G. Tuckey; the United Kingdom Atomic Energy Authority.

BIBLIOGRAPHY

The following is a brief selection from which specific works of science fiction have been excluded owing to their sheer number. Bibliographical details refer to the edition(s) consulted. Recommended to those wishing up-to-date information on military technology are *New Scientist* (UK) and *Aviation Week & Space Technology* (USA); relevant articles also appear occasionally in *Analog Science Fact/Science Fiction* and *Scientific American*.

Air Force Magazine (ed): *Space Weapons: a handbook of military astronautics* (Thames & Hudson, 1959)

Amis, Kingsley: *New Maps of Hell: a survey of science fiction* (Gollancz, 1960)

Asimov, Isaac: *Asimov on Astronomy* (Macdonald & Janes, 1974)

Asimov, Isaac: *Asimov's Guide to Science* (Basic Books, 1972; Penguin, 1975)

Asimov, Isaac: *The Tragedy of the Moon* (Abelard-Schuman, 1974)

Bergaust, Erik and Beller, William: *Satellite!* (Lutterworth, 1957)

Berry, Adrian: *The Iron Sun: crossing the universe through black holes* (Cape, 1977)

Berry, Adrian: *The Next Ten Thousand Years* (Cape, 1974)

Bester, Alfred: *The Life and Death of a Satellite* (Sidgwick & Jackson, 1967)

Brand, Stewart (ed): *Space Colonies* (Pelican, New York and London, 1977)

Brassey's Artillery of the World (Brassey's, 1977)

British Interplanetary Society: *Project Daedalus – Final Report* (British Interplanetary Society *Journal*, 1978)

Clarke, Arthur C. (ed): *The Coming of the Space Age* (Gollancz, 1967)

Clarke, Arthur C.: *Profiles of the Future* (Gollancz, 1962; revised edition, Gollancz, 1973)

Clarke, Arthur C.: *Report on Planet Three and other Speculations* (Gollancz, 1972)

Cox, John: *Overkill: the story of modern weapons* (Kestrel Books, 1976)

Davies, Paul: *the Runaway Universe* (Dent, 1978)

de Camp, L. Sprague: *Ancient Engineers* (Tandem, 1977)

Duncan, Ronald, and Weston-Smith, Miranda (eds): *The Encyclopaedia of Ignorance* (Pergamon Press, 1977)

Eiseley, Loren: *The Unexpected Universe* (Gollancz, 1970)

Ford, Brian: *German Secret Weapons* (1927; Ballantine Books, distributed by Pan Books, 1969)

Gamow, George: *Mr Tompkins in Paperback* (Cambridge University press, 1967)

Gibson, W. M.: *Nuclear Reactions* (Penguin, 1971)

Glasstone, S. (ed): *The Effects of Nuclear Weapons* (US Department of Defense, 1977)

Haldane, J. B. S. *A Banned Broadcast and other Essays* (Chatto & Windus, 1946)

Haldane, J. B. S.: *The Inequality of Man* (Chatto & Windus, 1932)

Haldane, J. B. S.: *Possible Worlds* (Chatto & Windus, 1927)

Hecht, Jeff: 'Laser Weapons: a status report', *Analog* 97 No 10 (1977)

Her Majesty's Stationery Office: *Nuclear Weapons* (1974)

Hughes, I. S.:*Elementary Particles* (Penguin, 1972)

Jane's Weapon Systems (Macdonald and Janes, 1978)

Jungk, Robert: *Brighter Than a Thousand Suns* (1958; Penguin, 1970)

Kahn, Herman: *On Escalation* (Princeton University Press, 1965)

Kahn, Herman: *On Thermonuclear War* (Princeton University Press, 1960)

Kahn, Herman: *Thinking About the Unthinkable* (Weidenfeld & Nicolson, 1962)

Langford, David: 'The Still Small Voice Inside', *Pulsar I* (Penguin, 1978)

Laurie, Peter: *Beneath the City Streets* (revised edition; Granada)

Machiavelli, Niccolò: *The Prince* (*Il Principe*) (Oxford University Press, 1935)

Nahin, P. J.: 'The Laser BMD', *Analog* 97 No 10 (1977)

Niven, Larry: 'Theory and Practice of Teleportation', (*Galaxy*, 1969)

Niven, Larry: 'Theory and Practice of Time Travel', *Vertex* 1 No 1 (1973)

O'Neill, Gerard: *The High Frontier: human colonies in space* (Morrow, 1976)

Rathjens, G. W., and Kistiakowsky, G. B.: 'The limitation of Strategic Arms', *Scientific American* 222 No 1 (1970)

Ridley, B. K. *Time, Space and Things* (Penguin, 1976)

Rorvik, David: *As Man Becomes Machine* (Souvenir Press, 1973)

Russell, Bertrand: *The Impact of Science on Society* (Allen & Unwin, 1952; AMS Press, 1953)

Sagan, Carl: *The Cosmic Connection: an extraterrestrial perspective* (Coronet Books, 1975)

Sagan, Carl: *Other Worlds* (Bantam Books, 1975)

Sagan, Carl, and Shklovskii, Iosif S.: *Intelligent Life in The Universe* (Holden-Day, 1966; Picador, 1977)

Smith & Sorokin: *The Laser* (McGraw-Hill, 1966)

Stableford, Brian: *The Mysteries of Modern Science* (Routledge & Kegan Paul, 1977)

Stoneley, Jack, with Lawton, A. T.: *Tunguska: Cauldron of Hell* (Star, 1977)

Sullivan, Walter: *We Are Not Alone: the search for intelligent life on other worlds* (1964; revised edition, Pelican, 1970)

Taylor, Gordon Rattray: *The Doomsday Book* (Thames & Hudson, 1970)

Taylor, John: *Black Holes: the end of the universe?* (Souvenir Press, 1973)

von Clausewitz, Carl: *On War (Vom Kriege)* (1832; reprinted Pelican, 1968)

von Neumann, John, and Morgenstern, Oskar: *Theory of Games and Economic Behaviour* (Princeton University Press, 1947; Oxford University Press, 1947)

Walters, Robert E.: *The Nuclear Trap* (Penguin, 1975)

Watson, James D.: *The Double Helix* (Weidenfeld & Nicolson, 1968)

Wheeler, John A. (ed): *Geometrodynamics* (Academic Press, London & New York, 1962)

INDEX